PRACTICING TO TAKE THE GRE® LITERATURE IN ENGLISH TEST

2nd Edition

INCLUDES:

- An actual GRE Literature in English Test administered in 1989-90
- Sample questions, instructions, and answer sheets
- Percent of examinees answering each question correctly

AN OFFICIAL PUBLICATION OF THE GRE BOARD

Published by Educational Testing Service
for the Graduate Record Examinations Board

The Graduate Record Examinations® Program offers a General Test measuring developed verbal, quantitative, and analytical abilities and Subject Tests measuring achievement in the following 16 fields:

Biochemistry, Cell and Molecular Biology	Economics	Literature in English	Political Science
Biology	Education	Mathematics	Psychology
Chemistry	Engineering	Music	Sociology
Computer Science	Geology	Physics	
	History		

The tests are administered by Educational Testing Service under policies determined by the Graduate Record Examinations Board, an independent board affiliated with the Association of Graduate Schools and the Council of Graduate Schools.

The Graduate Record Examinations Board has officially made available for purchase practice books, each containing a full-length test, for 15 of the Subject Tests. A practice book is not available for the Biochemistry, Cell and Molecular Biology Test at this time. Two General Test practice books are also available.

Individual booklets describing each test and including sample questions are available free of charge for all 16 Subject Tests. You may request these booklets by writing to:

Graduate Record Examinations
Educational Testing Service
P.O. Box 6014
Princeton, NJ 08541-6014

The Graduate Record Examinations Board and Educational Testing Service are dedicated to the principle of equal opportunity, and their programs, services, and employment policies are guided by that principle.

EDUCATIONAL TESTING SERVICE, ETS, the ETS logo, GRADUATE RECORD EXAMINATIONS, and GRE are registered trademarks of Educational Testing Service.

In association with Warner Books, Inc., a Warner Communications Company.

Copyright © 1992 by Educational Testing Service. All rights reserved.

USA: 0-446-39203-0
CAN: 0-446-39204-9

TABLE OF CONTENTS

BACKGROUND FOR THE TEST

Practicing to Take the GRE Literature in English Test 4
Additional Information 5
Purpose of the GRE Subject Tests 6
Development of the GRE Literature in English Test 6
Content of the GRE Literature in English Test 7
Sample Questions 10

TAKING THE TEST

Test-Taking Strategy 64
How to Score Your Test 65
Evaluating Your Performance 68
Practice GRE Literature in English Test, Form GR9064 71
Answer Sheets 135

BACKGROUND FOR THE TEST

PRACTICING TO TAKE THE GRE® LITERATURE IN ENGLISH TEST

This practice book has been published on behalf of the Graduate Record Examinations Board to help potential graduate students prepare to take the GRE Literature in English Test. The book contains the actual GRE Literature in English Test administered in October 1989, along with a section of sample questions, and includes information about the purpose of the GRE Subject Tests, a detailed description of the content specifications for the GRE Literature in English Test, and a description of the procedures for developing the test. All test questions that were scored have been included in the practice test.

The sample questions included in this practice book are organized by content category and represent the types of questions included in the test. The purpose of these questions is to provide some indication of the range of topics covered in the test as well as to provide some additional questions for practice purposes. These questions do not represent either the length of the actual test or the proportion of actual test questions within each of the content categories.

Before you take the full-length test, you may want to answer the sample questions. A suggested time limit is provided to give you a rough idea of how much time you would have to complete the sample questions if you were answering them on an actual timed test. After answering the sample questions, evaluate your performance within content categories to determine whether you would benefit by reviewing certain courses.

This practice book contains a complete test book, including the general instructions printed on the back cover and inside back cover. When you take the test at the test center, you will be given time to read these instructions. They show you how to mark your answer sheet properly and give you advice about guessing.

Try to take this practice test under conditions that simulate those in an actual test administration. Use the answer sheets provided on pages 135 to 142 and mark your answers with a No. 2 (soft-lead) pencil as you will do at the test center. Give yourself 2 hours and 50 minutes in a quiet place and work through the test without interruption, focusing your attention on the questions with the same concentration you would use in taking the test to earn a score. Since you will not be permitted to use them at the test center, do not use keyboards, dictionaries or other books, compasses, pamphlets, protractors, highlighter pens, rulers, slide rules, calculators (including watch calculators), stereos or radios with headphones, watch alarms including those with flashing lights or alarm sounds, or paper of any kind.

After you complete the practice test, use the work sheet and conversion tables on pages 66 and 67 to score your test. The work sheet also shows the estimated percent of GRE Literature in English Test examinees from a recent three-year period who answered each question correctly. This will enable you to compare your performance on the questions with theirs. Evaluating your performance on the actual test questions as well as the sample questions should help you determine whether you would benefit further by reviewing certain courses before taking the test at the test center.

We believe that if you use this practice book as we have suggested, you will be able to approach the testing experience with increased confidence.

ADDITIONAL INFORMATION

If you have any questions about any of the information in this book, please write to:

> Graduate Record Examinations
> Educational Testing Service
> P.O. Box 6000
> Princeton, NJ 08541-6000

PURPOSE OF THE GRE SUBJECT TESTS

The GRE Subject Tests are designed to help graduate school admission committees and fellowship sponsors assess the qualifications of applicants in their subject fields. The tests also provide students with an assessment of their own qualifications.

Scores on the tests are intended to indicate students' knowledge of the subject matter emphasized in many undergraduate programs as preparation for graduate study. Since past achievement is usually a good indicator of future performance, the scores are helpful in predicting students' success in graduate study. Because the tests are standardized, the test scores permit comparison of students from different institutions with different undergraduate programs.

The Graduate Record Examinations Board recommends that scores on the Subject Tests be considered in conjunction with other relevant information about applicants. Because numerous factors influence success in graduate school, reliance on a single measure to predict success is not advisable. Other indicators of competence typically include undergraduate transcripts showing courses taken and grades earned, letters of recommendation, and GRE General Test scores.

DEVELOPMENT OF THE GRE LITERATURE IN ENGLISH TEST

Each new edition of the Literature in English Test is developed by a committee of examiners composed of professors in the subject who are on undergraduate and graduate faculties in different types of institutions and in different regions of the United States. In selecting members for the committee of examiners, the GRE Program seeks the advice of the Modern Language Association of America.

The content and scope of each test are specified and reviewed periodically by the committee of examiners who, along with other faculty members who are also subject-matter specialists, write the test questions. All questions proposed for the test are reviewed by the committee and revised as necessary. The accepted questions are assembled into a test in accordance with the content specifications developed by the committee of examiners to ensure adequate coverage of the various aspects of the field and at the same time to prevent overemphasis on any single topic. The entire test is then reviewed and approved by the committee.

Subject-matter and measurement specialists on the ETS staff assist the committee of examiners, providing information and advice about methods of test construction and helping to prepare the questions and assemble the test. In addition, they review every test question to identify and eliminate language, symbols, or content considered to be potentially offensive, inappropriate, or serving to perpetuate any negative attitudes. The test as a whole is also reviewed to make sure that the test questions, where applicable, include an appropriate balance of people in different groups and different roles.

Because of the diversity of undergraduate curricula in this subject, it is not possible for a single test to cover all the material an examinee may have studied.

The examiners, therefore, select questions that test the basic knowledge and understanding most important for successful graduate study in the field. The committee keeps the test up-to-date by regularly developing new editions and revising existing editions. In this way, the test content changes steadily but gradually, much like most curricula.

When a new edition is introduced into the program, it is equated; that is, the scores are related by statistical methods to scores on previous editions so that scores from all editions in use are directly comparable. Although they do not contain the same questions, all editions of the Literature in English Test are constructed according to equivalent specifications for content and level of difficulty, and all measure equivalent knowledge and skills.

After a new edition of the Literature in English Test is first administered, examinees' responses to each test question are analyzed to determine whether the question functioned as expected. This analysis may reveal that a question is ambiguous, requires knowledge beyond the scope of the test, or is inappropriate for the group or a particular subgroup of examinees taking the test. Such questions are not counted in computing examinees' scores.

CONTENT OF THE GRE LITERATURE IN ENGLISH TEST

Each edition of the test contains approximately 230 questions on poetry, drama, biography, the essay, criticism, the short story, the novel, and, to a limited extent, the history of the language; some questions are based on short works reprinted in their entirety, some are excerpts from longer works. The test draws on English and American literature of all periods; it also contains a few questions on well-known writers from other countries and on works, including the Bible, translated from foreign languages. Throughout, the emphasis is on major authors, works, genres, and movements.

The questions may be somewhat arbitrarily classified into two groups: factual and critical. The factual questions test a student's knowledge of the major writers typically studied in college literature courses. For example, the student may be asked to identify a writer's chief contribution to literary history, to assign a literary work to the period in which it was written, to identify the primary theme of a work, to identify common kinds of poetic meter, to recognize a literary or classical allusion in a given context, to identify a writer or work described in a brief critical comment, or to determine the period or author of a work on the basis of the style and content of a short excerpt. The critical questions test the ability to read a literary text perceptively. Students are asked to examine a given passage of prose or poetry and to answer questions about the theme, meaning, form and structure, literary techniques, and various aspects of its language.

The approximate distribution of questions according to content categories is indicated by the following outline.

I. Literary Analysis (40-55%)
   Questions that require an ability to interpret given passages of prose and poetry. Such questions may involve recognition of conventions and genres, of allusions and references, and of meaning and tone.

II. Identification (20-25%)
    Identification of date, author, or work by style and/or content

III. Factual Information (20-25%)
     Factual questions on literary history and chronology, as well as identification of author or work through a critical statement or biographical information. Also identification of details of character, plot, or setting of a work.

IV. History and Theory of Literary Criticism (5-10%)

The literary-historical scope of the test follows the distribution below.

Literature to 1660	25-35%
English Literature 1660-1925	30-40%
American Literature before 1925	10-15%
British and American Literature after 1925	20-25%
Continental, Classical, and Comparative Literature	5-10%

Examinees may feel that the test has included or emphasized those areas in which they are least prepared. In fact, examinees tend to remember most vividly the questions that proved troublesome. Students taking the GRE should remember that in a test of this many questions much of the material presents no undue difficulty. The very length and scope of the examination eventually work to the benefit of students and give them an opportunity to demonstrate what they do know. No one is expected to answer all the questions correctly.

The committee of examiners is aware of the limitations of the multiple-choice format, particularly for testing competence in literary study. An examination of this kind provides no opportunity for the student to formulate a critical response or support a generalization, and, inevitably, it sacrifices depth to range of coverage. However, in a national testing program designed for a wide variety of students with differing preparations, the use of a large number of short, multiple-choice questions has proved to be the most effective and reliable way of providing a fair and valid examination.

The committee considers the test an instrument by which to offer *supplementary* information about students. In no way is the examination intended to minimize the importance of the students' college records or the recommendations of faculty members who have had the opportunity to work closely with the students. The committee assumes that those qualities and skills not measured by a national multiple-choice test are reflected in a student's academic record and recommendations. However, the test may help to place students in a national perspective or add another dimension to their profiles. The committee and ETS recommend that a test score not serve as the sole arbiter in the selection process or in decisions relating to scholarship assistance.

It should be noted that a test intended to meet the needs of a particular department should be constructed specifically to measure the knowledge and skills the department considers important. A standardized test, such as the GRE Literature in English Test, allows comparisons of students from different institutions with different programs on *one* measure of competence in English literature. Ideally, a department should not only investigate the relationships between the success of students in advanced study and several measures of competence, but also conduct a systematic evaluation of the test's predictive effectiveness after accumulating sufficient records of the graduate work of its students.

SAMPLE QUESTIONS

The sample questions included in this practice book are organized by content category and represent the types of questions included in the test. The purpose of these questions is to provide some indication of the range of topics covered in the test as well as to provide some additional questions for practice purposes. These questions do not represent either the length of the actual test or the proportion of actual test questions within each of the content categories. A time limit of 110 minutes is suggested to give you a rough idea of how much time you would have to complete the sample questions if you were answering them on an actual timed test. Correct answers to the sample questions are listed on page 63.

When you take the actual GRE test, you will be instructed to mark your answers on the separate answer sheet. The directions for the sample questions have been modified. For these questions, you may record your answers in one of two ways: 1) you can use the option bubbles at the bottom-right corner of each question or 2) you can use one of the sample answer sheets provided in this book.

Directions: Each of the questions or incomplete statements is followed by five suggested answers or completions. Select the one that is best in each case.

I. LITERARY ANALYSIS

Literature to 1660

Questions 1-4

> His comb was redder than the fin coral,
> And batailed, as it were a castel wal;
> His bile was blak, and as the jeet it shoon;
> Like asure were his legges, and his toon;
> His nailes whitter than the lilye flowr,
> And lik the burned gold was his colour.

1. The character being described by Chaucer is

   (A) joly Absolon (B) Chanticleer (C) Reynard the Fox
   (D) hende Nicholas (E) Pertelote

2. Which of the following has two syllables when the lines are properly read aloud?

   (A) "were" (line 2) (B) "bile" (line 3) (C) "jeet" (line 3)
   (D) "nailes" (line 5) (E) "flowr" (line 5)

3. In line 3, "bile" refers to his

   (A) beak (B) liver (C) food
   (D) eye (E) brush

4. The *n* in "toon" (line 4) is

   (A) part of the stem
   (B) a remnant of the Old English accusative
   (C) a sign of the plural
   (D) a dative plural ending
   (E) a sign of the strong declension

Questions 5-6

And that comyn englysshe that is spoken in one shyre varyeth from a nother. In so moche that in my dayes happened that certayn marchauntes were in a shippe in tamyse, for to have sayled over the see into zelande, and for lacke of wynde, thei taryed atte forlond, and wente to lande for to refreshe them. And one of theyme named Sheffelde, a mercer, cam in-to an hows and axed for mete; and specyally he axyd after eggys. And the goode wyf answerde, that she coude speke no frenshe. And the marchaunt was angry, for he also coude speke no frenshe, but wolde have hadde egges, and she understode hym not. And thenne at laste a nother sayd that he wolde have eyren. Then the good wyf sayd that she understod hym wel.

5. The merchants in the passage intended to go

  (A) across the Channel
  (B) across the Thames
  (C) across the Irish Sea
  (D) to the inland counties
  (E) to the western coast of England

6. The author relates an incident illustrating the

  (A) difficulties of traveling in a foreign country
  (B) attitude of English merchants toward countryfolk
  (C) varieties of dialects in common use in England
  (D) changing customs of the merchant class
  (E) shortages of food in the inland counties

7. ... as spices, the more they are beaten, the sweeter scent they send forth; or as the herb camomile, the more it is trodden down, the more it spreadeth abroad; so virtue and honesty, the more it is spited, the more it sprouteth and springeth.

  This passage illustrates the style best labeled as

  (A) Augustan (B) Petrarchan (C) Skeltonic
    (D) Swiftian (E) Euphuistic

8. Wherefore thinke on the doubtfull state of warres,
    Where Mars hath sway, he keepes no certayne course.
    Sometimes he lettes the weaker to prevaile,
    Sometimes the stronger stoupes: hope, feare, and rage
    With eylesse lott rules all, uncertayne good,
    Most certaine harmes, be his assured happes.

    Which of the following best summarizes the lines above?

    (A) Men are inherently malevolent and therefore justly punished by the gods.
    (B) The divine right of the ruler insures his eventual victory.
    (C) The meek shall eventually prevail, but they endure much suffering.
    (D) In a hostile universe, human prowess insures military victory.
    (E) In a world governed by chance, military victory does not necessarily come to those who deserve it.

    Ⓐ Ⓑ Ⓒ Ⓓ Ⓔ

Questions 9-10

An ant is a wise creature for itself, but it is a shrewd thing in an orchard or garden. And certainly men that are great lovers of themselves waste the public. Divide with reason between self love and society, and be so true to thyself as thou be not false to others. It is a poor center of a man's actions, himself. It is right earth. For that only stands fast upon his own center, whereas all things that have affinity with the heavens move upon the center of another, which they benefit.

9. To make his argument more convincing, the author uses

    (A) demonstrations of maximum utility
    (B) rational axioms of proper behavior
    (C) realistic facts of natural existence
    (D) images drawn from commerce and architecture
    (E) analogies from natural history and astronomy

    Ⓐ Ⓑ Ⓒ Ⓓ Ⓔ

10. The passage argues in favor of

    (A) selfishness
    (B) egotism
    (C) social consciousness
    (D) self-reliance
    (E) mass identity

    Ⓐ Ⓑ Ⓒ Ⓓ Ⓔ

11. My mistress' eyes are nothing like the sun;
    Coral is far more red than her lips' red;
    If snow be white, why then her breasts are dun;
    If hairs be wires, black wires grow on her head.

    The lines above express the speaker's

    (A) sense of the extravagance of some poetic conventions
    (B) sorrow at his inability to love most of the women he meets
    (C) awareness of his social inferiority to the lady he addresses
    (D) intention to end a love affair
    (E) self-delusion as to the beauty of his mistress

12.   How could communities,
    Degrees in schools and brotherhoods in cities,
    Peaceful commerce from dividable shores,
    The primogenitive and due of birth,
    Prerogative of age, crowns, sceptres, laurels,
    But by degree, stand in authentic place?

    These lines are most accurately described as a

    (A) justification of a constitutional society based on universal suffrage
    (B) commendation of a tyrannical society based on the great man theory of history
    (C) glorification of an atheistic society based on the survival of the fittest
    (D) plea for a democratic society based on common law
    (E) rationalization of a hierarchical society based on inherited privilege

13.   Methinks I hear
    Antony call: I see him rouse himself
    To praise my noble act; I hear him mock
    The luck of Caesar, which the gods give men
    To excuse their after wrath: husband, I come:
    Now to that name my courage prove my title!

    In these lines Cleopatra asserts that she will

    (A) prove herself a queen by seeking out Caesar
    (B) earn the right to call Antony "husband" by her suicide
    (C) rouse her armies by a stirring act of bravery
    (D) flee so that the field of battle is left to Antony and Caesar
    (E) deflect the "after wrath" of the gods from those she loves

Questions 14-18

When I have seen by Time's fell hand defaced
The rich, proud cost of outworn buried age;
When sometime lofty towers I see down-razed,
And brass eternal slave to mortal rage;
(5) When I have seen the hungry ocean gain
Advantage on the kingdom of the shore,
And the firm soil win of the watery main,
Increasing store with loss and loss with store;
When I have seen such interchange of state,
(10) Or state itself confounded to decay,
Ruin hath taught me thus to ruminate,
That Time will come and take my love away.
   This thought is as a death, which cannot choose
   But weep to have that which it fears to lose.

14. Which of the following lines conveys an idea similar to the idea in line 3?

   (A) I all alone beweep my outcast state
   (B) The fairest votary took up that fire
   (C) Love's fire heats water, water cools not fire
   (D) Like as the waves make toward the pebbled shore
   (E) And sable curls all silvered o'er with white

15. The subject of the main clause of the first sentence is

   (A) "I" (line 1)
   (B) "brass" (line 4)
   (C) "soil" (line 7)
   (D) "Ruin" (line 11)
   (E) "Time" (line 12)

16. The argument of lines 1-12 is based on

   (A) prejudice (B) testimony (C) probability
       (D) analogy (E) authority

17. A work showing a similar preoccupation with time is

    (A) Marlowe's *Hero and Leander*
    (B) Spenser's "Mutabilitie Cantos"
    (C) Donne's "The Ecstasy"
    (D) Jonson's "A Celebration of Charis"
    (E) Herbert's "The Pulley"

18. Which of the following is the best summary of the last two lines?

    (A) To weep is to be cowardly at the prospect of loss.
    (B) To weep is to be ungrateful for the mercy of death.
    (C) To think is to diminish the intensity of experience.
    (D) To love is to exist apart from the flux of experience.
    (E) To love is to know that one must experience loss.

Questions 19-21

> I gave to Hope a watch of mine: but he
>   An anchor gave to me.
> Then an old prayer-book I did present:
>   And he an optic sent.
> With that I gave a vial full of tears:
>   But he a few green ears.
> Ah loiterer! I'll no more, no more I'll bring:
>   I did expect a ring.

19. The speaker's offerings of "a watch," "a prayer-book," and "a vial of tears" represent his

    (A) antiquarian interests
    (B) love of earthly things
    (C) rejection of material possessions
    (D) discovery of scientific principles
    (E) long-time devotion and suffering

20. In responding with "an anchor," "an optic" (a telescope), and "a few green ears," Hope gives

    (A) advice on navigation
    (B) support for the virtues of country life
    (C) an earnest of future good
    (D) an omen of catastrophe
    (E) a warning against sin

21. The speaker's hoped-for reward, "a ring," represents

    (A) high social status
    (B) wealth
    (C) luck at games of chance
    (D) eternal union with God
    (E) the certainty of political recognition

English Literature 1660-1925

Questions 22-27

All is best, though we oft doubt,
What the unsearchable dispose
Of Highest Wisdom brings about,
And ever best found in the close.
(5) Oft He seems to hide His face,
But unexpectedly returns
And to His faithful champion hath in place
Bore witness gloriously; whence Gaza mourns,
And all that band them to resist
(10) His uncontrollable intent;
His servants He with new acquist
Of true experience from this great event
With peace and consolation hath dismissed,
And calm of mind, all passion spent.

22. Which is closest in meaning to the "unsearchable dispose" (line 2)?

    (A) Inscrutable design
    (B) Unrecognized glory
    (C) Irrecoverable grace
    (D) Misunderstood warnings
    (E) Lost power

23. Lines 1-4 of the poem imply that we

    (A) perceive the order and design of the universe because our wisdom and intellect allow us to do so
    (B) must question the wisdom of the universal order, even though we have only a limited understanding of the universe
    (C) must submit to a higher wisdom, even though that wisdom is erratic and destructive
    (D) offend God with our scientific probings into nature
    (E) should accept the universe as being wisely ordered, even though we are unable to understand it fully

24. Line 5 reinforces the meaning of

    (A) "All is best" (line 1)
    (B) "unsearchable dispose" (line 2)
    (C) "Highest Wisdom" (line 3)
    (D) "brings about" (line 3)
    (E) "in the close" (line 4)

25. Which of the following is the closest paraphrase of line 9?

    (A) And all who join together to oppose
    (B) And all of the oppositions they joined together against
    (C) And they oppose the band of
    (D) And they, set in opposition by that band,
    (E) And all those who opposed banding against

26. How is "His uncontrollable intent" (line 10) best rephrased?

    (A) His undirected thought
    (B) His unsurpassed strength
    (C) His outraged response
    (D) His irresistible will
    (E) His disorganized plan

27. The direct object of "hath dismissed" (line 13) is

    (A) "Gaza" (line 8)
    (B) "His servants" (line 11)
    (C) "He" (line 11)
    (D) "true experience" (line 12)
    (E) "peace and consolation" (line 13)

28. The idea that "might makes right" is stated in which of the following?

   (A) Treason doth never prosper; what's the reason?
   　　For if it prosper, none dare call it treason.
   (B) Power tends to corrupt, and absolute power corrupts absolutely.
   (C) Only That which made us meant us to be mightier by and by,
   　　Set the sphere of all the boundless heavens within the human eye.
   (D) 　Respecting man, whatever wrong we call,
   　　May, must be right, as relative to all.
   (E) How well her name an Army doth present,
   　　In whom the Lord of Hosts did pitch his tent!

   Ⓐ Ⓑ Ⓒ Ⓓ Ⓔ

Questions 29-31

   JONATHAN: My dear, I wish you would lie a little longer in bed
   　this morning.
   LAETITIA: Indeed I cannot; I am engaged to breakfast with
   　Jack Strongbow.
   JONATHAN: I don't know what Jack Strongbow doth so often at my
   　house. I assure you I am uneasy at it; for, though I have no suspicion
   　of your virtue, yet it may injure your reputation in the opinion of
   　my neighbors.
   LAETITIA: I don't trouble my head about my neighbors; and they shall no
   　more tell me what company I am to keep than my husband shall.

29. The best synonym for "virtue," as Jonathan uses that word, is

   (A) strength   (B) chastity   (C) goodness
   　(D) temperance   (E) fertility

   Ⓐ Ⓑ Ⓒ Ⓓ Ⓔ

30. The author chose the name Jack Strongbow because it suggests

   (A) avarice   (B) elegance   (C) honesty
   　(D) virility   (E) poverty

   Ⓐ Ⓑ Ⓒ Ⓓ Ⓔ

31. The dialogue is characteristic of

   (A) a medieval morality play
   (B) a Restoration comedy
   (C) a Tudor farce derived from a French original
   (D) an Elizabethan masque
   (E) an early American melodrama

   Ⓐ Ⓑ Ⓒ Ⓓ Ⓔ

32. Ring out ye Crystall spheres
    Once bless our human ears,
        (If ye have power to touch our senses so)
    And let your silver chime
    Move in melodious time;
        And let the Base of Heav'n's deep Organ blow,
    And with your ninefold harmony
    Make up full consort to th' Angelic symphony.

    In writing this stanza the poet assumes that his readers are familiar with the

    (A) musical theories of Aristotle
    (B) astronomical theories of Kepler
    (C) theology of St. Augustine
    (D) aesthetics of Longinus
    (E) cosmology of Ptolemy

Questions 33-36

    Fled are those times when, in harmonious strains,
    The rustic poet praised his native plains.
    No shepherds now, in smooth altérnate verse,
    Their country's beauty or their nymph's rehearse;
(5) Yet still for these we frame the tender strain,
    Still in our lays fond Corydons complain,
    And shepherds' boys their amorous pains reveal,
    The only pains, alas! they never feel.

33. The best paraphrase of "smooth altérnate" (line 3) is

    (A) predominantly alliterative
    (B) regularly metrical
    (C) full of sound symbolism
    (D) characterized by the juxtaposition of images
    (E) blank verse alternating with free verse

34. In this context, the best synonym for "rehearse" (line 4) is

    (A) revise   (B) prepare   (C) instruct
        (D) recite   (E) practice

35. Which of the following is the best synonym for "fond" (line 6)?

    (A) fundamental (B) lazy (C) doting
    (D) ecstatic (E) unhappy

36. The speaker is suggesting the irrelevance of

    (A) pastoral poetry (B) epic poetry
    (C) dramatic verse (D) patriotic odes
    (E) formal satire

37. This City now doth, like a garment, wear
    The beauty of the morning; silent, bare,
    Ships, towers, domes, theatres, and temples lie
    Open unto the fields, and to the sky;
    All bright and glittering in the smokeless air

    "This City" in line 1 is

    (A) London
    (B) New York
    (C) Paris
    (D) Canterbury
    (E) Edinburgh

Questions 38-41

England in 1819

An old, mad, blind, despised, and dying king —
Princes, the dregs of their dull race, who flow
Through public scorn — mud from a muddy spring;
Rulers who neither see, nor feel, nor know,
(5) But leechlike to their fainting country cling,
Till they drop, blind in blood, without a blow;
A people starved and stabbed in the untilled field —
An army, which liberticide and prey
Makes as a two-edged sword to all who wield;
(10) Golden and sanguine laws which tempt and slay;
Religion Christless, Godless — a book sealed;
A Senate — Time's worst statute unrepealed —
Are graves, from which a glorious Phantom may
Burst, to illumine our tempestuous day.

38. The king of line 1 is

   (A) William of Orange
   (B) George I
   (C) Edward VI
   (D) George III
   (E) George V

39. In the context of line 3, "muddy spring" is a metaphor for

   (A) the highly industrialized condition of England
   (B) the ruling monarch's derangement
   (C) a disagreeable, wet season of the year
   (D) the present ruling family's heritage and background
   (E) the deplorably low level of public morality and behavior

40. In context, "Golden" (line 10) is best understood as

   (A) equitable
   (B) beautiful
   (C) simple
   (D) valuable
   (E) materialistic

41. The poem consists of a single sentence whose main verb is

   (A) "Makes" (line 9)
   (B) "sealed" (line 11)
   (C) "unrepealed" (line 12)
   (D) "Are" (line 13)
   (E) "Burst" (line 14)

23

Questions 42-47

> If by dull rhymes our English must be chained,
>   And, like Andromeda, the Sonnet sweet
> Fettered, in spite of painèd loveliness;
> Let us find out, if we must be constrained,
> (5) Sandals more interwoven and complete
> To fit the naked foot of poesy;
> Let us inspect the lyre, and weigh the stress
> Of every chord, and see what may be gained
>   By ear industrious, and attention meet;
> (10) Misers of sound and syllable, no less
>   Than Midas of his coinage, let us be
> Jealous of dead leaves in the bay-wreath crown;
> So, if we may not let the Muse be free,
>   She will be bound with garlands of her own.

42. Which of the following is compared to Andromeda (line 2)?

    (A) "dull rhymes" (line 1)
    (B) "our English" (line 1)
    (C) "the Sonnet sweet" (line 2)
    (D) The speaker of the poem
    (E) The audience

43. "Sandals" (line 5) is the metaphorical equivalent of

    (A) theme (B) rhyme (C) tone
      (D) metaphor (E) allusions to myth

44. Grammatically, "ear industrious" and "attention meet" (line 9) have the same structure as

    (A) bus driver (B) fiendish glee (C) wheelbarrow
      (D) heir apparent (E) holy matrimony

24

45. The allusion to Midas (line 11) is relevant because Midas

   (A) was lavish and extravagant
   (B) was envious of the power of others
   (C) was unwilling to spend his wealth
   (D) accidentally injured his daughter
   (E) bitterly regretted that he had ever wished for wealth

46. Which of the following is the best paraphrase of "Jealous of" (line 12)?

   (A) Moderately in favor of
   (B) Particularly watchful for
   (C) Intolerant of rivals for
   (D) Envious of competitors for
   (E) Resentful of criticism of

47. The phrase "garlands of her own" (line 14) means

   (A) floral wreaths awarded for poetic excellence
   (B) decorous sentiments
   (C) native words rather than words of foreign origin
   (D) a form unrestricted by content
   (E) a form fitted to content

Questions 48-49

> Peace, peace! he is not dead, he doth not sleep —
> He hath awakened from the dream of life —
> 'Tis we who, lost in stormy visions, keep
> With phantoms an unprofitable strife,
> And in mad trance strike with our spirit's knife
> Invulnerable nothings. — We decay
> Like corpses in a charnel; fear and grief
> Convulse us and consume us day by day,
> And cold hopes swarm like worms within our living clay.

48. Which of the following is represented as illusory in the lines above?

   (A) The visionary ideal
   (B) Life after death
   (C) The human spirit
   (D) Everyday existence
   (E) The mastery of spirit over flesh

49. The verse form is that of

    (A) blank verse
    (B) rhyme royal
    (C) a Spenserian stanza
    (D) an Elizabethan ballad
    (E) an English sonnet

Questions 50-52

   An article as necessary to a lady in this position as her brougham or her
bouquet, is her companion. I have always admired the way in which the
tender creatures, who cannot exist without sympathy, hire an exceedingly
plain friend of their own sex from whom they are almost inseparable.
(5) The sight of that inevitable woman in her faded gown seated behind her
dear friend in the opera-box, or occupying the back seat of the barouche, is
always a wholesome and moral one to me, as jolly a reminder as that of the
Death's-head which figured in the repasts of Egyptian bon-vivants, a
strange sardonic memorial of Vanity Fair. What? — even battered, brazen,
(10) beautiful, conscienceless, heartless Mrs. Firebrace, whose father died of her
shame: even lovely, daring Mrs. Mantrap, who will ride at any fence which
any man in England will take, and who drives her greys in the Park, while
her mother keeps a huxter's stall in Bath still; — even those who are so
bold, one might fancy they could face anything, dare not face the world
(15) without a female friend. They must have somebody to cling to, the affec-
tionate creatures! And you will hardly see them in any public place without
a shabby companion in a dyed silk, sitting somewhere in the shade close
behind them.

50. In the context of the paragraph, the main function of such phrases as
    "tender creatures" (line 3) and "dear friend" (line 6) is to

    (A) show the author's weakness for feminine charm
    (B) expose ironically the physical ugliness of the women
    (C) demonstrate the author's concern for the unfortunate
    (D) suggest the distance between appearance and reality
    (E) suggest the esteem in which the companions
        are held

51. Which of the following best describes the tone of the narrator?

    (A) Hearty and blustering
    (B) Sympathetic and good-natured
    (C) Understated and hesitant
    (D) Impersonal and detached
    (E) Insinuating and ironic

52. The passage suggests that ladies hire a companion in order to

    (A) assist a fellow creature who is in financial straits
    (B) set off their own beauty and emphasize their feminine fragility
    (C) remind others of their obligations to fellow creatures who may be lonely
    (D) make life easier for aging parents who can no longer act as chaperones
    (E) share their lives with a worthy friend who can serve them as a moral example

Questions 53-55

> Márgarét, áre you gríeving
> Over Goldengrove unleaving?
> Leáves, líke the things of man, you
> With your fresh thoughts care for, can you?
> Áh! ás the heart grows older
> It will come to such sights colder
> By and by, nor spare a sigh
> Though worlds of wanwood leafmeal lie;
> And yet you wíll weep and know why.
> Now no matter, child, the name:
> Sórrow's spríngs áre the same.
> Nor mouth had, no nor mind, expressed
> What heart heard of, ghost guessed:
> It ís the blight man was born for,
> It is Margaret you mourn for.

53. The word "unleaving" (line 2) emphasizes the

    (A) active process of autumnal decay
    (B) inevitability of springtime renewal
    (C) variety of beautiful forms in the natural world
    (D) reaction of nature to human attempts to control it
    (E) permanence of natural objects despite contrary appearances

54. Which of the following is the closest synonym for "fresh" (line 4)?

    (A) honorable (B) unkind (C) amused
    (D) young (E) disrespectful

55. The last two lines convey metaphorically the concept of

    (A) the divine origin of beauty
    (B) the evils of self-pity
    (C) the universality of death
    (D) the susceptibility to temptation
    (E) Platonic love

Questions 56-57

>   Move him into the sun —
>   Gently its touch awoke him once,
>   At home, whispered of fields unsown.
>   Always it woke him, even in France,
>   Until this morning and this snow.
>   If anything might rouse him now
>   The kind old sun will know.
>
>   Think how it wakes the seeds —
>   Woke, once, the clays of a cold star.
>   Are limbs, so dear-achieved, are sides,
>   Full-nerved — still warm — too hard to stir?
>   Was it for this the clay grew tall?
>   — O what made fatuous sunbeams toil
>   To break earth's sleep at all?

Wilfred Owen, "Futility." The work is covered by copyright and is reprinted by permission of the copyright owner.

56. The "him" in line 1 is

    (A) a victorious athlete
    (B) a fallen soldier
    (C) a crippled rebel
    (D) a sunbathing tourist
    (E) an inebriated farmer

57. The poem contrasts the

    (A) malevolence of the universe with the good will of men
    (B) ordinary lives of most men with the exploits of heroes
    (C) brutality inherent in nature with the gentle comforts of civilization
    (D) agonies of birth and life with the peacefulness of death
    (E) regenerative power of the sun with the implacable finality of death

58. Fielding, driven out of the trade of Molière and Aristophanes, took to that of Cervantes; and since then the English novel has been one of the glories of literature, whilst the English drama has been its disgrace. The extinguisher which Walpole dropped on Fielding descends on me in the form of the Lord Chamberlain's Examiner of Plays, a gentleman who robs and insults me as irresistibly as if he were the Tsar of Russia and I the meanest of his subjects.

    In the passage above, Shaw is

    (A) commenting on the effects of censorship
    (B) discussing the pervasive influence of the Encyclopedists
    (C) commenting on the snobbery of the typical English audience
    (D) discussing the generic differences between drama and the novel
    (E) acknowledging the superiority of Continental literature to English literature

American Literature before 1925

Questions 59-60

> Tis as you see nought but the Spoiles of Death,
> Gods High Controler and Impartial Taker;
> Free hold wee had of Land but none of Breath,
> All one day must resigne unto their Maker.

59. The above is

    (A) an ode (B) an apostrophe (C) an epitaph
    (D) a ballad (E) a refrain

    Ⓐ Ⓑ Ⓒ Ⓓ Ⓔ

60. Grammatically, line 2 is best described as

    (A) nouns in direct address
    (B) the direct object of *see*
    (C) in apposition with *you*
    (D) in apposition with *Death*
    (E) an adjective phrase modifying *Maker*

    Ⓐ Ⓑ Ⓒ Ⓓ Ⓔ

Questions 61-63

When we speak of nature in this manner, we have a distinct but most poetical sense in the mind. We mean the integrity of impression made by manifold natural objects. It is this which distinguishes the stick of timber of the wood-cutter from the tree of the poet. The charming landscape which I
(5) saw this morning is indubitably made up of some twenty or thirty farms. Miller owns this field, Locke that, and Manning the woodland beyond. But none of them owns the landscape. There is a property in the horizon which no man has but he whose eye can integrate all the parts, that is, the poet. This is the best part of these men's farms, yet to this their warranty-
(10) deeds give no title.

61. In the context of the paragraph, the wood-cutter's "stick of timber" is distinguished from the poet's "tree" in that the

    (A) integrity of the tree is violated by the wood-cutter's axe
    (B) "tree" is a useless object, whereas the "stick of timber" is useful
    (C) "stick" has been cut off the tree, whereas the "tree" itself is still growing
    (D) poet sees objects in their organic unity, whereas the wood-cutter notices only their parts
    (E) wood-cutter's occupation is to destroy nature, whereas the poet's obligation is to preserve it

62. Which of the following best describes the word "property" in line 7?

    (A) It is a personification.
    (B) It is part of a simile.
    (C) It creates an antithesis.
    (D) It has a double meaning.
    (E) It makes a Biblical allusion.

63. The passage above is from

    (A) Crèvecoeur's *Letters from an American Farmer*
    (B) Coleridge's *Biographia Literaria*
    (C) Carlyle's *Past and Present*
    (D) Paine's *Common Sense*
    (E) Emerson's *Nature*

Questions 64-65

And, maddened with despair so that he laughed loud and long, did Goodman Brown grasp his staff and set forth again, at such a rate that he seemed to fly along the forest path rather than to walk or run. The road grew wilder and drearier and more faintly traced, and vanished at length,
(5) leaving him in the heart of the dark wilderness, still rushing onward with the instinct that guides mortal man to evil.

64. The "dark wilderness" (line 5) is a metaphor for

    (A) the spiritual exercises leading to grace
    (B) hopefulness about the future
    (C) depravity in the inner self
    (D) the rewards of continence
    (E) faith in the order of nature

65. The author of the passage above is also the author of

    (A) *The Sound and the Fury*
    (B) *The Scarlet Letter*
    (C) *The Deerslayer*
    (D) *Benito Cereno*
    (E) *The Red Badge of Courage*

Questions 66-68

Yet Do I Marvel

I doubt not God is good, well-meaning, kind,
And did He stoop to quibble could tell why
The little buried mole continues blind,
Why flesh that mirrors Him must some day die,
Make plain the reason tortured Tantalus
Is baited by the fickle fruit, declare
If merely brute caprice dooms Sisyphus
To struggle up a never-ending stair.
Inscrutable His ways are, and immune
To catechism by a mind too strewn
With petty cares to slightly understand
What awful brain compels His awful hand.
Yet do I marvel at this curious thing:
To make a poet black, and bid him sing!

"Yet Do I Marvel" from *On These I Stand* by Countee Cullen. Copyright, 1925 by Harper & Row, Publishers, Inc.; renewed, 1953 by Ida M. Cullen. Used by permission of the publishers.

66. Which of the following most closely restates the speaker's view of God?

    (A) God is just but vindictive.
    (B) God need not inspire a poet to create a poem.
    (C) God is benevolent and merciful to all living things.
    (D) God's intentions are beyond human understanding.
    (E) The ways of God can be explained only in metaphorical language.

    Ⓐ Ⓑ Ⓒ Ⓓ Ⓔ

67. The poem differs in form from the kind of English sonnet that Shakespeare wrote in that

    (A) its turning point comes after the first quatrain
    (B) it uses imperfect rhyme
    (C) it reverses the usual order of the sestet and octave
    (D) it ends in a couplet
    (E) it substitutes couplets for the third quatrain

    Ⓐ Ⓑ Ⓒ Ⓓ Ⓔ

68. This sonnet is concerned with what philosophers call the

    (A) appeal to prejudice and ignorance
    (B) hasty generalization from irrelevant evidence
    (C) use of syllogistic reasoning
    (D) problem of evil in the universe
    (E) conventional approach to religious belief

    Ⓐ Ⓑ Ⓒ Ⓓ Ⓔ

British and American Literature after 1925

Questions 69-72

　　　Obscurely yet most surely called to praise,
　　　As sometimes summer calls us all, I said
　　　The hills are heavens full of branching ways
　　　Where star-nosed moles fly overhead the dead;
(5)　I said the trees are mines in air, I said
　　　See how the sparrow burrows in the sky!
　　　And then I wondered why this mad <u>instead</u>
　　　Perverts our praise to uncreation, why
　　　Such savor's in this wrenching things awry.
(10)　Does sense so stale that it must needs derange
　　　The world to know it? To praiseful eye
　　　Should it not be enough of fresh and strange
　　　That trees grow green, and moles can course in clay,
　　　And sparrows sweep the ceiling of our day?

　　　　　　From *The Beautiful Changes and Other Poems*, copyright 1947, 1975 by
　　　　　　Richard Wilbur. Reprinted by permission of Harcourt Brace Jovanovich, Inc.

69. Which of the following is closest in meaning to "this mad <u>instead</u>" (line 7)?

    (A) The call to praise
    (B) The irrational behavior of the sparrow
    (C) The transience of summer's beauty
    (D) The compulsion to use metaphor
    (E) The confused images of day and night

70. The repetition of the phrase "I said" (lines 2 and 5) serves to emphasize the fact that the

    (A) subject of the poem is the speaker's response to the situation
    (B) listener is challenging the speaker's statements
    (C) speaker makes an objective factual report on the scene described in line 6
    (D) speaker wishes to duplicate the effect of a ballad refrain
    (E) speaker is alone and unable to forget his solitary state

71. Which of the following best describes the last two lines of the poem?

    (A) They demonstrate the effectiveness of factual descriptions.
    (B) They stress that the source of praise is obscure.
    (C) They make an objective factual report on the situation described in line 6.
    (D) They reveal an organic unity in nature.
    (E) They gradually revert to metaphorical language.

72. Which of the following ideas is implicit in the poem?

    (A) One reads poetry not merely in terms of one's own sensibilities but in terms of the prejudices and daydreams that one brings to a poem.
    (B) Poetry is not a turning loose of emotion, but an escape from emotion; it is not the expression of personality, but an escape from personality.
    (C) The literature of sentiment and emotion must go; it cheats us into a sense of involvement with life and society; it makes us believe we can "take arms against a sea of troubles."
    (D) The writer is both anarchist and architect; his dreams sap and rebuild the provisional landscape of reality. He comes to poetry for its singular capacity to "dream against the world," to structure worlds that are otherwise.
    (E) A Poet, as he is the author to others of the highest wisdom, pleasures, virtues, and glory, so he ought personally to be the happiest, the best, the wisest, and the most illustrious of men.

Questions 73-75

Standing to America, bringing home
black gold, black ivory, black seed.

> *Deep in the festering hold thy father lies,*
> *of his bones New England pews are made,*
> *those are altar lights that were his eyes.*

73. The poem from which the passage above is taken is about

    (A) coal mining
    (B) oil exploration
    (C) the slave trade
    (D) the colonization of New England
    (E) the homecoming of war veterans

74. The tone of lines 3-5 may best be described as one of

    (A) jubilant exhortation
    (B) optimistic nostalgia
    (C) factual description
    (D) moral outrage
    (E) amused sarcasm

75. Lines 3-5 are a reworking of a song in Shakespeare's

    (A) *Cymbeline* (B) *The Tempest* (C) *A Winter's Tale*
    (D) *Twelfth Night* (E) *As You Like It*

76. Honour, high honour, and renown,
    To Hymen, god of every town!

    A refrain like this would appear most appropriately in an

    (A) epitaph (B) epithalamium (C) epigram
    (D) elegy (E) encomium

Questions 77-78

I'm a wormy hermit in a country of prize pigs so corn-happy they can't see the slaughterhouse at the end of the track. I'm Jeremiah vision-bitten in the Land of Cockaigne.

77. What is the relationship between the two sentences?

    (A) They are related as in a chronological sequence.
    (B) The second sentence contradicts the first.
    (C) They express similar ideas in different images.
    (D) The first sentence states a cause and the second an effect of that cause.
    (E) The second sentence presents a detail supporting the generalization in the first.

78. Which of the following is from another description of the Land of Cockaigne (line 3)?

(A) Of sugar cakes are the shingles all,
Of church, of cloister, bower and hall;
The pinnacles are fat puddings,
Fit to be served to princes and kings

(B) Now — the country does not even boast a tree,
    As you see,
To distinguish slopes of verdure, certain rills
    From the hills

(C)   . . . a darkling plain
Swept with confused alarms of struggle and flight,
Where ignorant armies clash by night

(D) The woods decay, the woods decay and fall,
The vapors weep their burthen to the ground,
Man comes and tills the field and lies beneath,
And after many a summer dies the swan

(E) Much have I traveled in the realms of gold,
And many goodly states and kingdoms seen

Continental, Classical, and Comparative Literature

79. Apollo gave oracular responses nine days a year, once each month except in winter (when Dionysus took over the oracle). The visitors had to be dealt with one by one, but the more important the inquirer the more likely it was that he would be seen early. Sophocles seems to have taken great care, in the account of the patricide, to preserve verisimilitude concerning the one-day-a-month responses. When Oedipus and Laius meet on the road between Thebes and Delphi, Oedipus has just received a response and Laius is probably on the way to place a request. Sophocles specifies a spot that is close enough to Delphi so that both men might have been dealt with on the same day. Laius, however, may well have been in some haste to arrive in time.

    In the discussion above, the critic is attempting to

    (A) provide stage directions for a performance of Sophocles' *Oedipus*
    (B) provide information that will minimize the improbability of one element in the Oedipus story
    (C) demonstrate the role of the *deus ex machina* in a typical Greek tragedy
    (D) explain the effect of the events of Sophocles' *Oedipus* on the Greek audience
    (E) explain the workings of *hubris* as both a motivational force and as an element in the denouement

    Ⓐ Ⓑ Ⓒ Ⓓ Ⓔ

80. In a certain Chinese encyclopedia it is written that animals are divided into (a) belonging to the Emperor, (b) embalmed, (c) tamed, (d) suckling pigs, (e) sirens, (f) fabulous, (g) dogs at liberty, (h) included in the present classification, (i) which act like madmen, (j) innumerable, (k) drawn with a very fine camel's hair brush, (l) et cetera, (m) which have just broken jugs, (n) which from afar look like flies.

    In the lines above, Borges attempts to

    (A) protest the intellectual restraints upon writers living under a totalitarian regime
    (B) suggest, by allegory, similarities between people and animals
    (C) provide an exotic system of thought that suggests the weaknesses of logical classifications
    (D) make a serious contribution to our understanding of metaphor
    (E) dramatize the failure in communication among scientists

    Ⓐ Ⓑ Ⓒ Ⓓ Ⓔ

II. IDENTIFICATION

Questions 81-93

For each of the following passages, identify the author or the work. Base your decision on the content and style of each passage.

81. And if ye stand in doute
     Who brought this ryme aboute,
     My name is Colyn Cloute.
     I purpose to shake oute
     All my connyng bagge,
     Lyke a clerkely hagge;
     For though my ryme be ragged,
     Tattered and iagged,
     Rudely rayne beaten,
     Rusty and moughte eaten,
     If you take well therwith,
     It hath in it some pyth.

   (A) Geoffrey Chaucer (B) John Skelton (C) Edmund Spenser
      (D) Ben Jonson (E) Andrew Marvell

   Ⓐ Ⓑ Ⓒ Ⓓ Ⓔ

82. September 29, 1662: This day my oaths for drinking of wine and going to plays are out, and so I do resolve to take a liberty today, and then to fall to them again. To the King's Theatre, where we saw "Midsummer's Night's Dream," which I had never seen before, nor shall ever again, for it is the most insipid ridiculous play that ever I saw in my life. I saw, I confess, some dancing and some handsome women, which was all my pleasure.

   (A) Dryden (B) Pope (C) Pepys
      (D) Swift (E) Lamb

   Ⓐ Ⓑ Ⓒ Ⓓ Ⓔ

83. . . . two of his servants, the learned Poggius and a friend, ascended the Capitoline Hill, reposed themselves among the ruins of columns and temples, and viewed from that commanding spot the wide and various prospect of desolation. The place and the object gave ample scope for moralizing on the vicissitudes of fortune, which spares neither man nor the proudest of his works, which buries empires and cities in a common grave.

    (A) Defoe
    (B) Lyly
    (C) Spenser
    (D) Jonson
    (E) Gibbon

84. When we came upon Highgate hill and had a view of London, I was all life and joy. I repeated Cato's soliloquy on the immortality of the soul, and my soul bounded forth to a certain prospect of happy futurity. I sung all manner of songs, and began to make one about an amorous meeting with a pretty girl, the burthen of which was as follows:

    She gave me this, I gave her that;
    And tell me, had she not tit for tat?

    I gave three huzzas, and we went briskly in.

    (A) Boswell (B) Johnson (C) Addison
        (D) Gibbon (E) Pope

85. The shadow of the dome of pleasure
    Floated midway on the waves;
    Where was heard the mingled measure
    From the fountain and the caves.
    It was a miracle of rare device,
    A sunny pleasure dome with caves of ice!

    (A) Crashaw (B) Donne (C) Coleridge
        (D) Wallace Stevens (E) Hart Crane

86. You cannot paint or sing yourself into being good men; you must be good men before you can either paint or sing, and then the colour and sound will complete in you all that is best.

    (A) Wilde (B) Poe (C) T. S. Eliot
        (D) Ruskin (E) Orwell

87. Things fall apart; the center cannot hold;
    Mere anarchy is loosed upon the world,
    The blood-dimmed tide is loosed, and everywhere
    The ceremony of innocence is drowned.

    (A) "Among School Children"
    (B) "The Lake Isle of Innisfree"
    (C) "The Wild Swans at Coole"
    (D) "The Second Coming"
    (E) "Crazy Jane Talks with the Bishop"

88. A rat crept softly through the vegetation
    Dragging its slimy belly on the bank
    While I was fishing in the dull canal
    On a winter evening round behind the gashouse
    Musing upon the king my brother's wreck.

    (A) Pound
    (B) Hart Crane
    (C) T. S. Eliot
    (D) Browning
    (E) Auden

89. They were careless people, Tom and Daisy — they smashed up things and creatures and then retreated back into their money or their vast carelessness, or whatever it was that kept them together, and let other people clean up the mess they had made.

    (A) Fitzgerald's *The Great Gatsby*
    (B) Faulkner's *Light in August*
    (C) Dreiser's *An American Tragedy*
    (D) James's *The Golden Bowl*
    (E) Baldwin's *Giovanni's Room*

90. Unless it can be proven to me — to me as I am now today, with my heart and my beard, and my putrefaction — that in the infinite run it does not matter a jot that a North American girl-child named Dolores Haze had been deprived of her childhood by a maniac, unless that can be proven (and if it can, then life is a joke), I see nothing for the treatment of my misery, but the melancholy and very local palliative of articulate art.

(A) Nabokov's *Lolita*
(B) Roth's *Goodbye, Columbus*
(C) Malamud's *The Assistant*
(D) Pynchon's *V.*
(E) Waugh's *Vile Bodies*

91. I shall know why — when Time is over —
And I have ceased to wonder why —
Christ will explain each separate anguish
In the fair schoolroom of the sky —

He will tell me what "Peter" promised —
And I — for wonder at his woe —
I shall forget the drop of Anguish
That scalds me now — that scalds me now!

(A) Pound (B) Keats (C) Housman
   (D) Stephen Crane (E) Emily Dickinson

92. "That is the person who shot my son."
"My dear, how too shattering for you. Not dead, I hope? Chokey shot a man at a party the other night. He gets gay at times, you know. It's only when he's on his best behaviour that he's so class-conscious. I must go and rescue the Vicar."

(A) D. H. Lawrence (B) James Joyce (C) Virginia Woolf
   (D) Evelyn Waugh (E) Joseph Conrad

93. Far from my mother and grandmother, my bedroom became the fixed point on which my melancholy and anxious thoughts were centered. Someone had had the happy idea of giving me, to distract me on evenings when I seemed abnormally wretched, a magic lantern . . . it substituted for the opaqueness of my walls an impalpable iridescence, supernatural phenomena of many colours, in which legends were depicted, as on a shifting and transitory window.

    (A) Dostoevski   (B) Colette   (C) Mann
       (D) Zola   (E) Proust

94. It was with the sense of a, for him, very memorable something that he peered now into the immediate future, and tried, not without compunction, to take up that period where he had, prospectively, left it. But just where the deuce had he left it? The consciousness of dubiety was, for our friend, not, this morning, quite yet clean-cut enough to outline the figures on what she had called his horizon, between which and himself the twilight was indeed a quality somewhat intimidating.

    The author parodied is

    (A) Nathaniel Hawthorne   (B) Henry James   (C) Edith Wharton
       (D) Mark Twain   (E) Herman Melville

95. I profess . . . that I have not the least personal interest in endeavouring to promote this necessary work, having no other motive than the *public good of my country, by advancing our trade, providing for infants, relieving the poor, and giving some pleasure to the rich.*

    This passage is from the concluding paragraph of a work by

    (A) Bacon   (B) Hazlitt   (C) Dryden
       (D) Lamb   (E) Swift

96. His verse, I confess, is not harmonious to us, but . . . they who lived with him and some time after him thought it musical. There is the rude sweetness of a Scotch tune in it, which is natural and pleasing, though not perfect. 'Tis true, I cannot go so far as he who published the last edition of him; for he would make us believe the fault is in our ears, and that there were really ten syllables in a verse where we find but nine: but this opinion is not worth confuting; 'tis so gross and obvious an error, that common sense (which is a rule in everything but matters of faith and revelation) must convince the reader, that equality of numbers in every verse which we call heroic, was either not known, or not always practised in his age.

    The passage above was written by

    (A) Dryden about Chaucer
    (B) Coleridge about Milton
    (C) Johnson about Donne
    (D) Arnold about Wordsworth
    (E) Pope about Spenser

97. All fleeth save Good-Deeds, and that am I . . .
    Fear not, I will speak for thee . . .
    Let us go and never come again.

    The quotation above is from

    (A) *The Spanish Tragedy*
    (B) *The Shoemaker's Holiday*
    (C) *Everyman*
    (D) *Volpone*
    (E) *Tamburlaine*

Questions 98-100 refer to the following excerpts from autobiographical narratives.

98. Which is by F. Scott Fitzgerald?

99. Which is by Flannery O'Connor?

100. Which is by Ezra Pound?

(A)   When I read in memoirs about the Paris of the Steins, Sylvia Beach, Joyce, and Hemingway, I am cast down. I was there. I may have passed them in the street; I had simply never heard of them. Nor had I any notion of what they were trying to do. I had really carried my isolation in England with me.

(B)   I knew at 15 pretty much what I wanted to do. I believed that the "impulse" to write is with the gods, but that technique is a writer's own responsibility. I resolved that at 30 I would know more about poetry than anyone living, that I would know the dynamic content from the shell. In this search I learned more or less of nine foreign languages. I read Oriental stuff in translations, I fought every university regulation and every professor who tried to make me learn anything except this, or who bothered me with "requirements for degrees."

(C)   I found myself in a millstream of gregariousness in New York and London: incessant contact with great theatre stars, with rich people and social people, at posh hotels, at parties, and on yachts. But through it all I never shook off the plaintive counterpoint of my parents, their religion and their poverty.

(D)   In preparatory school and up to the middle of sophomore year in college, it worried me that I wasn't going and hadn't gone to Yale. Was I missing a great American secret? There was a gloss upon Yale that Princeton lacked; Princeton's flannels hadn't been pressed for a week, its hair always blew a little in the wind. Nothing was ever carried through at Princeton with the same perfection as the Yale Junior Prom or the elections to their senior societies.

(E)   Whenever I'm asked why Southern writers particularly have a penchant for writing about freaks, I say it is because we are still able to recognize one. To be able to recognize a freak, you have to have some conception of the whole man, and in the South the conception of the whole man is still, in the main, theological . . . I think it is safe to say that while the South is hardly Christ-centered it is most certainly Christ-haunted. . . . Ghosts can be very fierce and instructive. They cast strange shadows.

III. FACTUAL INFORMATION

Questions 101-103 refer to the descriptions below.

101. Which describes the masque?

    Ⓐ Ⓑ Ⓒ Ⓓ Ⓔ

102. Which describes the medieval mystery play?

    Ⓐ Ⓑ Ⓒ Ⓓ Ⓔ

103. Which describes the commedia dell'arte?

    Ⓐ Ⓑ Ⓒ Ⓓ Ⓔ

(A) On a platform erected in the town square was a line of settings ranging from the throne of God at one end to the mouth of Hell at the other. The performers in this drama moved along this stage enacting each scene before an appropriate facade, while the audience stood before the stage or observed from the windows of neighboring buildings.

(B) With texts by such poets as Ben Jonson, spectacular costumes and settings by architects like Inigo Jones, and music by distinguished composers, these works were performed by and for members of the royal family and their aristocratic guests.

(C) These travelling players depended more on their stereotyped costumes and masks than on scenery. They had a repertory of short "scenarios" which could be combined in many ways since the overall stories varied little and the dialogue was at least partly extemporized. Each player specialized in a specific role, such as Pantalone, the avaricious old man, or Harlequin, the clever servant.

(D) The plays and their performance are conventionalized in even the smallest detail. The stage setting always remains the same. Some of the main features are a panel with a painting of an old pine tree; on one side of the stage a bridge to a curtained doorway; over the stage a roof with four corner pillars; and at the back, four musicians.

(E) The performances took place in the great halls of castles between courses of long banquets. The works were more skits or debates than plays, and they dealt, often in facetious exaggerations of legal or philosophical quibbling, with such topics as the different types of weather.

104. The heroine of this travesty of flowery romanticism eludes her blind and jealous husband by meeting her lover in a pear tree. No dreamy, swooning heroine, she is a quick-witted young woman perfectly able to turn to her own advantage even so unpromising a situation as her husband's regaining his sight at an extremely inconvenient moment.

    The heroine described above appears in

    (A) The Knight's Tale
    (B) The Merchant's Tale
    (C) The Prioress's Tale
    (D) The Clerk's Tale
    (E) The Parson's Tale

105. The relationship between *Richard II* and Holinshed's *Chronicles* is most closely paralleled by the relationship between

    (A) Bacon's and Montaigne's *Essays*
    (B) *Absalom and Achitophel* and *Aesop's Fables*
    (C) *Julius Caesar* and Plutarch's *Lives*
    (D) Donne's poems and Petrarch's sonnets
    (E) *Paradise Lost* and *Paradise Regained*

106. . . . and, when he shall die,
    Take him and cut him out in little stars,
    And he will make the face of heaven so fine
    That all the world will be in love with night
    And pay no worship to the garish sun.

    These lines are spoken by

    (A) Juliet about Romeo
    (B) Miranda about Ferdinand
    (C) Cordelia about Lear
    (D) Portia about Bassanio
    (E) Beatrice about Benedick

107. And thorns shall come up in her palaces, nettles and brambles in the fortresses thereof: and it shall be an habitation of dragons and a court of owls. The wild beasts of the desert shall also meet with the wild beast of the island, and the satyr shall cry to his fellow; the screech owl also shall rest there, and find for herself a place of rest.

The speaker of this prophecy is

(A) Shylock (B) Roland (C) Isaiah
(D) Jesus (E) Beowulf

108. _____ , childless, rich, feigns sick, despairs,
Offers his state to hopes of several heirs,
Lies languishing; his parasite receives
Presents of all, assures, deludes; then weaves
Other cross plots, which ope themselves, are told,
New tricks for safety are sought, they thrive; when bold
Each tempts the other again, and all are sold.

Which of the following correctly completes line 1?

(A) Volpone
(B) Tamburlaine
(C) Mosca
(D) Malvolio
(E) Coriolanus

109. Therefore is the name of it called _____; because the Lord did there confound the language of all the earth: and from thence did the Lord scatter them abroad upon the face of all the earth.

Which of the following correctly completes the sentence above?

(A) Babylon (B) Mount Sinai (C) Babel
(D) Jerusalem (E) Bethlehem

110. While rarely pointing the finger of morality, the author means us to know how differently a man behaves toward those he considers his equals and those he considers his inferiors. He notes the disparity between man commanding his pleasures and man attempting to please, and the divergence, in the case of sex, between seeing a woman as a wench and contemplating her for a wife. With zest, style, and good humor he has made a comedy sensitive to the nuances of class and caste.

    The play under discussion is

    (A) Dryden's *All for Love*
    (B) Goldsmith's *She Stoops to Conquer*
    (C) O'Casey's *Juno and the Paycock*
    (D) Ibsen's *Hedda Gabler*
    (E) Chekhov's *The Cherry Orchard*

111. He was a determinist, perhaps rather a fatalist, who depicted the strivings and passions of individuals as being in conflict with inexorable processes in the world. The heath, the village with its peasants, meant as much to him, perhaps, as the characters, many of them women, that he so convincingly created. He was a poet as well as a novelist.

    The author described is

    (A) George Meredith
    (B) Charles Dickens
    (C) Thomas Hardy
    (D) D. H. Lawrence
    (E) Anthony Trollope

112. In her dying delirium she cries out against being "Mrs. Linton, the lady of Thrushcross Grange, and the wife of a stranger; an exile, and outcast . . . from what had been my world. . . . I wish I were a girl again, half savage and hardy, and free . . . and laughing at injuries, not maddening under them! Why am I so changed?"

    The character described is

    (A) Tess in *Tess of the D'Urbervilles*
    (B) Becky Sharp in *Vanity Fair*
    (C) Catherine Earnshaw in *Wuthering Heights*
    (D) Hester Prynne in *The Scarlet Letter*
    (E) Eppie in *Silas Marner*

Questions 113-115 refer to the excerpts below.

113. In which is the "I" George Eliot's Maggie Tulliver?
Ⓐ Ⓑ Ⓒ Ⓓ Ⓔ

114. In which is the "I" Jane Austen's Emma Woodhouse?
Ⓐ Ⓑ Ⓒ Ⓓ Ⓔ

115. In which is the "I" Defoe's Moll Flanders?
Ⓐ Ⓑ Ⓒ Ⓓ Ⓔ

(A) I wish we could have been friends — I mean, if it would have been good and right for us. But that is the trial I have to bear in everything: I may not keep anything I used to love when I was little. The old books went; and Tom is different — and my father. It is like death. I must part with everything I cared for when I was a child. And I must part with you: we must never take any notice of each other again. That was what I wanted to speak to you for. I wanted to let you know that Tom and I can't do as we like about such things.

(B) I have escaped; and that I should escape, may be a matter of grateful wonder to you and my self. But this does not <u>acquit</u> him, Mrs. Weston; and I must say, that I think him greatly to blame. What right had he to come among us with affection and faith engaged, and with manner so very disengaged? What right had he to endeavour to please, as he certainly did — to distinguish any one young woman with persevering attention, as he certainly did — while he really belonged to another? — How could he tell what mischief he might be doing? — How could he tell that he might not be making me in love with him? — very wrong, very wrong indeed.

(C) Do you think I can stay to become nothing to you? Do you think I am an automaton? — a machine without feelings? and can bear to have my morsel of bread snatched from my lips, and my drop of living water dashed from my cup? Do you think, because I am poor, obscure, plain, and little, I am soulless and heartless? You think wrong! I have as much soul as you — and full as much heart! and if God had gifted me with some beauty and much wealth, I should have made it as hard for you to leave me, as it is now for me to leave you.

50

(D) I love Willoughby, sincerely love him; and suspicion of his integrity cannot be more painful to yourself than to me. It has been involuntary, and I will not encourage it. I was startled, I confess, by the alteration in his manners this morning; — he did not speak like himself, and did not return your kindness with any cordiality. But all this may be explained by such a situation of his affairs as you have supposed. He had just parted from my sister, had seen her leave him in the greatest affliction.

(E) My Colour came and went at the sight of the Purse, and with the fire of his Proposal together, so that I could not say a Word, and he easily perceiv'd it; so putting the Purse in my Bosom, I made no more Resistance to him, but let him do just what he pleas'd, and as often as he pleas'd; and thus I finish'd my own destruction at once, for from this Day, being forsaken of my Virtue, and my Modesty, I had nothing of Value left to recommend me, either to God's Blessing, or Man's Assistance.

Questions 116-117

The _____ myth is that the work of art is a spontaneous and partially unconscious crystallization of feelings too deep and intense to be released directly into action. It is a myth so powerful that it can, at moments, create a reality when there is none at hand. _____ and many others were condemned to live out in later years the literary roles they had created for themselves with their earliest works; they read these works into their lives.

116. Which of the following correctly completes the first sentence?

(A) Classical
(B) Neoclassical
(C) Romantic
(D) Victorian
(E) Metaphysical

117. Which of the following correctly begins the third sentence?

(A) Johnson, Gibbon, Voltaire
(B) Byron, Chateaubriand, Goethe
(C) Arnold, Spengler, Balzac
(D) Hobbes, Pope, Diderot
(E) Yeats, Chekhov, Sartre

118. theyre all so different Boylan talking about the shape of my foot he noticed at once even before he was introduced when I was in the D B C with Poldy laughing and trying to listen I was waggling my foot we both ordered 2 teas and plain bread and butter . . .

The speaker is

(A) Milly Theale in *The Wings of the Dove*
(B) Rhoda in *The Waves*
(C) Emma in *Madame Bovary*
(D) Gudrun in *Women in Love*
(E) Molly Bloom in *Ulysses*

119. All that most maddens and torments; all that stirs up the lees of things; all truth with malice in it; all that cracks the sinews and cakes the brain; all the subtle demonism of life and thought; all evil to crazy _____, were visibly personified, and made practically assailable in _____.

Which of the following correctly completes the sentence above?

(A) Prospero . . . Caliban
(B) Ahab . . . Moby Dick
(C) K . . . the Castle
(D) Ike McCaslin . . . the Bear
(E) Hepzibah Pyncheon . . . the House of the Seven Gables

120. A central precept of the New England philosophy of transcendentalism is the belief in the

(A) "good life" as one which automatically provides the greatest good for the greatest number
(B) value of science to the discovery of truth, which is unchanging and unchangeable
(C) importance of the natural as opposed to the supernatural in controlling human destiny
(D) struggle of human beings with and against nature and each other
(E) unity of spirit and the world, and the immanence of spirit in the world

121. Born in Africa, _____ acquired in an incredibly short time both the literary culture and religion of her New England owners. Her writings reflect little of her homeland and much of the age in which she lived.

   Which of the following correctly completes the first sentence?

   (A) Anne Bradstreet (B) Anne Hutchinson (C) Phillis Wheatley
   (D) Isak Dinesen (E) Eudora Welty

122. In his writings, the concept of American individualism was pushed toward its limits. His views of government were somewhat anarchistic, and he insisted that if an injustice of government "is of such a nature that it requires injustice to another [you should] break the law, and let your life be a counter friction to stop the machine."

   The writer referred to is

   (A) Jonathan Edwards
   (B) Benjamin Franklin
   (C) Cotton Mather
   (D) Henry David Thoreau
   (E) Washington Irving

123. Pray for me! I reckoned if she knowed me she'd take a job that was more nearer her size. But I bet she done it, just the same — she was just that kind. She had the grit to pray for Judus if she took the notion — there warn't no back-down to her, I judge. You may say what you want to, but in my opinion she had more sand in her than any girl I ever see; in my opinion she was just full of sand. It sounds like flattery, but it ain't no flattery.

   The narrator is

   (A) Huckleberry Finn (B) Leopold Bloom (C) Daniel Deronda
   (D) Natty Bumppo (E) Holden Caulfield

124. "Mosque," "Caves," and "Temple" are the titles of the principal parts of

   (A) Voltaire's *Candide*
   (B) Forster's *A Passage to India*
   (C) Mann's *The Magic Mountain*
   (D) Proust's *Swann's Way*
   (E) Conrad's *Heart of Darkness*

125. My politician would be — or at least I was groping toward some such formulation — a man whose personal motivation had been, in one sense, idealistic, who in many ways was to serve the cause of social betterment, but who was corrupted by power, even by power exercised against corruption. That is, his means defile his ends. But more than that, he was to be a man whose power was based on the fact that somehow he could vicariously fulfill some secret needs of the people about him.

Which of the following accurately describes the passage above?

(A) Thomas Pynchon is discussing *Gravity's Rainbow*.
(B) John Updike is discussing *Rabbit, Run*.
(C) Ralph Ellison is discussing *Invisible Man*.
(D) Saul Bellow is discussing *Humboldt's Gift*.
(E) Robert Penn Warren is discussing *All the King's Men*.

126. It is a blasphemy-haunted but unblinking play in which the god Dionysus compels men to recognize his orgiastic presence within themselves — whether they wish to admit to anything so irrational or not.

The play referred to above is

(A) Sophocles' *Oedipus Rex*
(B) Sophocles' *Antigone*
(C) Aeschylus' *Prometheus Bound*
(D) Aristophanes' *Lysistrata*
(E) Euripides' *The Bacchae*

127. Such varied practitioners of the Renaissance love sonnet as Wyatt, du Bellay, Spenser, Daniel, and Shakespeare found a common inspiration in the poems of

(A) Catullus (B) Dante (C) Petrarch (D) Tasso (E) Sappho

128. *Madame Bovary* starts with little Charles Bovary's hat. We, his school-fellows (the only narrative use of the first person in the book), greeted the new boy and his silly hat with howls of laughter. "We" are society, and from this moment, Charles Bovary's nature — his timidity, indecision, lack of character — is fixed and the suicide many years later of his wife inexorably preordained.

The critic is dealing with Flaubert's attempt to

(A) portray the role of happenstance and chance in human events
(B) salvage intractable material by making it theatrically comic
(C) transform an absurd scene into a series of ironic revelations
(D) show that the work of art is a personal document unintelligible to anyone except the author
(E) construct a deterministically ordered chain of events

129. Feed the budding rose of boyhood with the drainage of your sewer;
Send the drain into the fountain, lest the stream should issue pure.

Set the maiden fancies wallowing in the troughs of Zolaism, —
Forward, forward, ay, and backward, downward too into the abyss!

The phrase "troughs of Zolaism" (line 3) refers to the

(A) political activities of European journalists
(B) excesses of the American and French Revolutions
(C) nature poets' overidealization of the beauties of the countryside
(D) romantic novel's excessive sentimentality and lack of social concern
(E) naturalistic novel's preoccupation with brutality and sexuality

130. Fear of women and of their sexuality is a masculine neurosis that precedes even Christianity, which sometimes gets blamed for it. The story of _____ embodies that terror.

Which of the following correctly completes the quotation above?

(A) the Sibyl and Lethe in the *Aeneid*
(B) the fox and the crow in *Aesop's Fables*
(C) the sirens and Circe in the *Odyssey*
(D) Grendel and his dam in *Beowulf*
(E) Jacob and Esau in the Old Testament

131. I maintain that all great men or even men a little out of the common, that is to say capable of giving some new word, must from their very nature be criminals.

The "I" of the passage above is

(A) Iago   (B) Emma Bovary   (C) Hedda Gabler
 (D) Captain Ahab   (E) Raskolnikov

IV. HISTORY AND THEORY OF LITERARY CRITICISM

132. The tragedies of the Athenian poets are as mirrors in which the spectator beholds himself, under a thin disguise of circumstance, stript of all but that ideal perfection and energy which every one feels to be the internal type of all that he loves, admires, and would become. The imagination is enlarged by a sympathy with pains and passions so mighty, that they distend in their conception the capacity of that by which they are conceived; the good affections are strengthened by pity, indignation, terror and sorrow; and an exalted calm is prolonged from the satiety of this high exercise of them into the tumult of familiar life: even crime is disarmed of half its horror and all its contagion by being represented as the fatal consequence of the unfathomable agencies of nature; error is thus divested of its wilfulness; men can no longer cherish it as the creation of their choice.

In the passage above, Shelley is discussing

(A) the sublime   (B) the dramatic unities   (C) the *deus ex machina*
 (D) *hamartia*   (E) *catharsis*

Questions 133-135 refer to the excerpts below.

133. In which does the author describe "false wit"?

134. In which does the author describe "true wit"?

135. In which does the author describe "metaphysical wit"?

56

(A) [It] chiefly consists in the resemblance and congruity sometimes of single letters, as in anagrams, chronograms, lipograms, and acrostics; sometimes of syllables, as in echoes and doggerel rhymes; sometimes of words, as in puns and quibbles.

(B) .   .   . Nature to advantage dressed,
What oft was thought, but ne'er so well expressed;

(C) The most heterogeneous ideas are yoked by violence together; nature and art are ransacked for illustrations, comparisons, and allusions.

(D) It is the Divine Vision not of The World nor of Man nor from Man as he is a Natural Man but only as he is a Spiritual Man. It has nothing to do with Memory.

(E) [It] is . . . an imitation of characters of lower type — not, however, in the full sense of the word bad, the ludicrous being merely a subdivision of the ugly.

136. The objection arising from the impossibility of passing the first hour at *Alexandria*, and the next at *Rome*, supposes, that when the play opens, the spectator really imagines himself at *Alexandria*, and believes that his walk to the theatre has been a voyage to *Egypt*, and that he lives in the days of *Antony and Cleopatra*. Surely he that imagines this may imagine more.

Which of the following accurately characterizes the passage above?

(A) It repudiates a strict use of the unities.
(B) It suggests that factual accuracy is crucial in historical plays.
(C) It insists on decorum as an element in tragedy.
(D) It asserts the desirability of giving English plays foreign settings.
(E) It rejects mixed genres.

137. "A confusion of actual meteorological conditions with the weather in the soul" is a playful definition of

(A) dramatic irony
(B) negative capability
(C) the pathetic fallacy
(D) the *deus ex machina*
(E) the objective correlative

Questions 138-140 refer to the excerpts below.

138. Which is by Arnold?

      Ⓐ Ⓑ Ⓒ Ⓓ Ⓔ

139. Which is by Sidney?

      Ⓐ Ⓑ Ⓒ Ⓓ Ⓔ

140. Which is by Wilde?

      Ⓐ Ⓑ Ⓒ Ⓓ Ⓔ

(A) Greek art, again, Greek beauty, have their root in the same impulse to see things as they really are, inasmuch as Greek art and beauty rest on fidelity to nature — the <u>best</u> nature — and on a delicate discrimination of what this best nature is. To say we work for sweetness and light, then, is only another way of saying that we work for Hellenism.

(B) It is justly considered as the greatest excellency of art, to imitate nature; but it is necessary to distinguish those parts of nature which are most proper for imitation: greater care is still required in representing life, which is so often discoloured by passion, or deformed by wickedness.

(C) Nature never set forth the earth in so rich tapestry as divers poets have done — neither with pleasant rivers, fruitful trees, sweet-smelling flowers, nor whatsoever else may make the too much loved earth more lovely. Her world is brazen, the poets only deliver a golden.

(D) A work that aspires, however humbly, to the condition of art should carry its justification in every line. And art itself may be defined as a single-minded attempt to render the highest kind of justice to the visible universe, by bringing to light the truth, manifold and one, underlying its every aspect.

(E) Where, if not from the Impressionists, do we get those wonderful brown fogs that come creeping down our streets, blurring the gaslamps and changing the houses into monstrous shadows? To whom if not to them and their master, do we owe the lovely silver mists that brood over our river, and turn to faint forms of fading grace, curved bridge and swaying barge? The extraordinary change that has taken place in the climate of London during the last ten years is entirely due to this particular school of Art.

141. In theory, a man could liberate himself by releasing those aboriginal feelings which had not yet been consigned to the Bastille of statutory forms and categories. Mostly those feelings provided poets with a night-school of dreams, fantasy, and chance. The motto for this undertaking was Lautréamont's famous elucidation of beauty as the casual meeting of a sewing machine and an umbrella on a dissecting table. In their day-classes poets invented relationships for the sole reason that they did not exist in nature. Breton said, "He who still refuses to see a horse galloping on a tomato should be looked upon as a cretin."

In the lines above a critic is describing

(A) existentialism (B) expressionism (C) surrealism
   (D) Freudianism (E) utilitarianism

Ⓐ Ⓑ Ⓒ Ⓓ Ⓔ

Questions 142-143

Great passions may give us this quickened sense of life, ecstasy and sorrow of love, the various forms of enthusiastic activity, disinterested or otherwise, which come naturally to many of us. Only be sure it is passion — that it does yield you this fruit of a quickened, multiplied consciousness. Of such wisdom, the poetic passion, the desire of beauty, the love of art for its own sake, has most. For art comes to you proposing frankly to give nothing but the highest quality to your moments as they pass, and simply for those moments' sake.

142. Which of the following is the best paraphrase of the passage?

(A) The artist is a higher creature than the spectator of art.
(B) Art helps us to perceive the spiritual element in life.
(C) Disinterested passions may grow from transitory enthusiasms.
(D) Aesthetic experience permits the greatest intensification of each moment.
(E) Eat, drink, and be merry, for tomorrow we die.

Ⓐ Ⓑ Ⓒ Ⓓ Ⓔ

143. The author is

(A) Johnson (B) Pater (C) Arnold
   (D) Hopkins (E) Ruskin

Ⓐ Ⓑ Ⓒ Ⓓ Ⓔ

144. He attacked "the heresy of the didactic" — the prevalent stress on moralizing in literature — and defined poetry as "the rhythmical creation of beauty."

The author described above is

(A) John Dryden
(B) Henry Wadsworth Longfellow
(C) Edgar Allen Poe
(D) Alexander Pope
(E) William Wordsworth

Ⓐ Ⓑ Ⓒ Ⓓ Ⓔ

Questions 145-146

The only way of expressing emotion in the form of art is by finding an "objective correlative"; in other words, a set of objects, a situation, a chain of events which shall be the formula of that <u>particular</u> emotion; such that when the external facts, which must terminate in sensory experience, are given, the emotion is immediately evoked.

145. The author is

(A) T. S. Eliot   (B) I. A. Richards   (C) W. B. Yeats
(D) Northrop Frye   (E) John Crowe Ransom

Ⓐ Ⓑ Ⓒ Ⓓ Ⓔ

146. This dictum has been used by its author to explain what he regards as the artistic failure of

(A) *Everyman*   (B) *The Prelude*   (C) *Paradise Lost*
(D) the *Divine Comedy*   (E) *Hamlet*

Ⓐ Ⓑ Ⓒ Ⓓ Ⓔ

147. There are others of the moderns who rival him in every other part of poetry; but in the greatness of his sentiments he triumphs over all the poets both modern and ancient, Homer only excepted. It is impossible for the imagination of man to distend itself with greater ideas, than those which he has laid together in his first, second and sixth books. The seventh, which describes the Creation of the World, is likewise wonderfully sublime, though not so apt to stir up emotion in the mind of the reader, nor consequently so perfect in the epic way of writing.

    The passage above exemplifies the application of critical concepts set forth by

    (A) Plato
    (B) Aristotle
    (C) Longinus
    (D) Horace
    (E) Cicero

148. The book is an uneasy combination of bold speculations about the origins of tragedy, brilliant reflections on Socrates (it is the first anti-Socratic book by a philosopher), and a call for the revitalization of Germany through the art of a new Aeschylus, Richard Wagner.

    The author of the book described above is

    (A) Freud (B) Voltaire (C) Camus
      (D) Goethe (E) Nietzsche

Questions 149-150

> The poet makes himself a *seer* by a long, prodigious, and rational *disordering* of *all the senses*. Every form of love, of suffering, of madness; he searches himself, he consumes all the poisons in him, and keeps only their quintessences. This is an unspeakable torture during which he needs all his faith and superhuman strength, and during which he becomes the great patient, the great criminal, the great accursed — and the great learned one! — among men. — For he arrives at the *unknown*! Because he has cultivated his own soul — which was rich to begin with — more than any other man! He reaches the unknown, and even if, crazed, he ends up by losing the understanding of his visions, at least he has seen them! Let him die charging through those unutterable, unnameable things: other horrible workers will come; they will begin from the horizons where he has succumbed! . . . So, then, the poet really is the thief of fire.

149. The allusion in the last line suggests that the poet

   (A) pits himself against the gods themselves
   (B) allows himself the comforts of home and hearth
   (C) must learn to discipline and deny his impulses
   (D) subordinates his vision to the immutable laws of nature
   (E) absorbs sense phenomena and then retires to order the flux of experience

150. The author is

   (A) Rimbaud
   (B) Racine
   (C) Goethe
   (D) Hugo
   (E) Voltaire

SAMPLE QUESTIONS ANSWER KEY

I. LITERARY ANALYSIS

Literature to 1660

1. B
2. D
3. A
4. C
5. A
6. C
7. E
8. E
9. E
10. C
11. A
12. E
13. B
14. E
15. D
16. D
17. B
18. E
19. E
20. C
21. D

English Literature (1660-1925)

22. A
23. E
24. B
25. A
26. D
27. B
28. A
29. B
30. D
31. B
32. E
33. B
34. D
35. C
36. A
37. A
38. D
39. D
40. E
41. D
42. C
43. B
44. D
45. C
46. B
47. E
48. D
49. C
50. D
51. E
52. B
53. A
54. D
55. C
56. B
57. E
58. A

American Literature before 1925

59. C
60. D
61. D
62. D
63. E
64. C
65. B
66. D
67. E
68. D

British & American Literature after 1925

69. D
70. A
71. E
72. D
73. C
74. D
75. B
76. B
77. C
78. A

Continental, Classical, Etc.

79. B
80. C

II. IDENTIFICATION

81. B
82. C
83. E
84. A
85. C
86. D
87. D
88. C
89. A
90. A
91. E
92. D
93. E
94. B
95. E
96. A
97. C
98. D
99. E
100. B

III. FACTUAL INFORMATION

101. B
102. A
103. C
104. B
105. C
106. A
107. C
108. A
109. C
110. B
111. C
112. C
113. A
114. B
115. E
116. C
117. B
118. E
119. B
120. E
121. C
122. D
123. A
124. B
125. E
126. E
127. C
128. E
129. E
130. C
131. E

IV. HISTORY & THEORY OF LITERARY CRITICISM

132. E
133. A
134. B
135. C
136. A
137. C
138. A
139. C
140. E
141. C
142. D
143. B
144. C
145. A
146. E
147. C
148. E
149. A
150. A

TAKING THE TEST
TEST-TAKING STRATEGY

Presumably, if you are about to take the GRE Literature in English Test, you are nearing completion of or have completed an undergraduate curriculum in that subject. A general review of your curriculum is probably the best preparation for taking the test. Because the level of difficulty of the test is set to provide reliable measurement over a broad range of subject matter, you are not expected to be able to answer every question correctly.

You are strongly urged to work through some of the sample questions preceding this section. After you have evaluated your performance within the content categories, you may determine that a review of certain courses would be to your benefit.

In preparing to take the full-length Literature in English Test, it is important that you become thoroughly familiar with the directions provided in the full-length test included in this book. For this test, your score will be determined by subtracting one-fourth the number of incorrect answers from the number of correct answers. Questions for which you mark no answer or more than one answer are not counted in scoring. If you have some knowledge of a question and are able to rule out one or more of the answer choices as incorrect, your chances of selecting the correct answer are improved, and answering such questions is likely to improve your score. It is unlikely that pure guessing will raise your score; it may lower your score.

Work as rapidly as you can without being careless. *This includes checking frequently to make sure you are marking your answers in the appropriate rows on your answer sheet.* Since no question carries greater weight than any other, do not waste time pondering individual questions you find extremely difficult or unfamiliar.

You may find it advantageous to go through the test a first time quite rapidly, stopping only to answer those questions of which you are confident. Then go back and answer the questions that require greater thought, concluding with the very difficult questions, if you have time.

HOW TO SCORE YOUR TEST

Total Subject Test scores are reported as three-digit scaled scores with the third digit always zero. The maximum possible range for all Subject Test total scores is from 200 to 990. The actual range of scores for a particular Subject Test, however, may be smaller. Literature in English Test scores typically range from 300 to 740. The range for different editions of a given test may vary because different editions are not of precisely the same difficulty. The differences in ranges among different editions of a given test, however, usually are small. This should be taken into account, especially when comparing two very high scores. In general, differences between scores at the 99th percentile should be ignored. **The score conversions table provided shows the score range for this edition of the test only.**

The work sheet on page 66 lists the correct answers to the questions. Columns are provided for you to mark whether you chose the correct (C) answer or an incorrect (I) answer to each question. Draw a line across any question you omitted, because it is not counted in the scoring. At the bottom of the page, enter the total number correct and the total number incorrect. Divide the total incorrect by 4 and subtract the resulting number from the total correct. This is the adjustment made for guessing. Then round the result to the nearest whole number. This will give you your raw total score. Use the total score conversion table to find the scaled total score that corresponds to your raw total score.

Example: Suppose you chose the correct answers to 175 questions and incorrect answers to 46. Dividing 46 by 4 yields 11.5. Subtracting 11.5 from 175 equals 163.5, which is rounded to 164. The raw score of 164 corresponds to a scaled score of 660.

WORK SHEET for the LITERATURE IN ENGLISH Test, Form GR9064 ONLY
Answer Key and Percentages* of Examinees Answering Each Question Correctly

QUESTION Number	Answer	P+	TOTAL C	TOTAL I	QUESTION Number	Answer	P+	TOTAL C	TOTAL I	QUESTION Number	Answer	P+	TOTAL C	TOTAL I
1	C	74			81	A	41			161	E	71		
2	D	90			82	C	47			162	A	46		
3	E	24			83	D	78			163	E	44		
4	C	72			84	D	49			164	B	12		
5	B	83			85	B	45			165	D	29		
6	A	54			86	E	50			166	A	38		
7	C	59			87	C	77			167	C	33		
8	E	88			88	D	58			168	E	41		
9	B	59			89	D	46			169	C	13		
10	A	88			90	A	29			170	B	21		
11	D	62			91	C	44			171	A	79		
12	C	90			92	B	36			172	C	57		
13	D	85			93	E	63			173	A	62		
14	E	27			94	E	31			174	D	32		
15	B	49			95	E	57			175	E	28		
16	A	60			96	D	80			176	C	85		
17	D	17			97	C	79			177	A	91		
18	E	47			98	B	57			178	E	85		
19	A	24			99	A	46			179	C	61		
20	D	27			100	D	79			180	B	42		
21	C	45			101	E	65			181	A	33		
22	B	95			102	A	54			182	D	45		
23	E	68			103	C	53			183	B	30		
24	B	42			104	B	83			184	B	45		
25	C	57			105	A	67			185	E	13		
26	B	58			106	E	35			186	D	33		
27	A	90			107	C	33			187	E	12		
28	B	52			108	D	54			188	B	12		
29	D	92			109	C	73			189	B	65		
30	E	64			110	A	79			190	C	45		
31	D	55			111	E	32			191	A	78		
32	B	83			112	E	72			192	D	35		
33	A	47			113	B	61			193	D	61		
34	C	88			114	C	25			194	E	14		
35	D	61			115	D	40			195	A	80		
36	B	37			116	B	61			196	A	42		
37	C	32			117	B	30			197	A	18		
38	A	23			118	A	45			198	B	41		
39	E	43			119	C	79			199	C	49		
40	C	77			120	C	73			200	B	56		
41	E	89			121	C	54			201	E	35		
42	A	44			122	D	66			202	D	36		
43	D	83			123	E	49			203	B	29		
44	D	50			124	E	32			204	E	73		
45	B	57			125	A	57			205	A	51		
46	B	92			126	D	37			206	E	51		
47	E	96			127	B	81			207	C	43		
48	C	48			128	D	73			208	B	33		
49	D	72			129	C	73			209	E	29		
50	A	62			130	E	66			210	A	37		
51	D	46			131	A	15			211	D	19		
52	E	41			132	C	48			212	C	80		
53	B	51			133	D	24			213	B	34		
54	A	55			134	C	34			214	D	56		
55	C	38			135	B	65			215	E	40		
56	A	82			136	D	34			216	B	88		
57	D	28			137	D	42			217	D	74		
58	E	74			138	B	51			218	E	58		
59	C	43			139	E	48			219	D	69		
60	D	90			140	A	39			220	B	18		
61	B	84			141	E	35			221	A	38		
62	A	75			142	C	43			222	B	60		
63	E	92			143	E	91			223	D	69		
64	D	47			144	A	87			224	E	54		
65	A	44			145	D	66			225	C	79		
66	B	83			146	C	39			226	A	38		
67	A	68			147	E	46			227	E	32		
68	C	43			148	B	29			228	A	29		
69	E	64			149	B	44			229	B	43		
70	B	73			150	E	41			230	C	39		
71	D	70			151	C	69							
72	A	54			152	D	61							
73	D	65			153	A	19							
74	A	28			154	C	58							
75	B	26			155	D	15							
76	A	75			156	E	38							
77	C	19			157	B	29							
78	E	86			158	B	23							
79	A	72			159	C	64							
80	E	64			160	A	74							

Correct (C) _____

Incorrect (I) _____

Total Score:

C − I/4 = _____

Scaled Score (SS) = _____

*The P+ column lists the percent of an analysis sample of Literature in English Test examinees who answered each question correctly; this sample consists of October 1989 examinees selected to represent all Literature in English Test examinees tested between October 1, 1986, and September 30, 1989.

SCORE CONVERSIONS AND PERCENTS BELOW*
FOR GRE LITERATURE IN ENGLISH TEST, Form GR9064 ONLY

TOTAL SCORE					
Raw Score	Scaled Score	%	Raw Score	Scaled Score	%
230	830	99	91-94	490	33
226-229	820	99	87-90	480	30
222-225	810	99	83-86	470	26
217-221	800	99	79-82	460	23
213-216	790	99	75-78	450	20
209-212	780	99	71-74	440	17
205-208	770	99	67-70	430	14
201-204	760	99	63-66	420	12
197-200	750	99	59-62	410	10
193-196	740	99	55-58	400	8
189-192	730	99	51-54	390	7
185-188	720	98	47-50	380	5
181-184	710	98	42-46	370	4
177-180	700	97	38-41	360	3
173-176	690	96	34-37	350	3
169-172	680	94	30-33	340	2
165-168	670	93	26-29	330	2
161-164	660	91	22-25	320	1
156-160	650	89	18-21	310	1
152-155	640	87	14-17	300	1
148-151	630	85	10-13	290	0
144-147	620	82	6-9	280	0
140-143	610	79	2-5	270	0
136-139	600	76	0-1	260	0
132-135	590	73			
128-131	580	69			
124-127	570	66			
120-123	560	62			
116-119	550	58			
112-115	540	54			
108-111	530	49			
104-107	520	45			
99-103	510	41			
95-98	500	37			

*Percent scoring below the scaled score based on the performance of 20,956 examinees who took the GRE Subject Test in Literature in English between October 1, 1986, and September 30, 1989.

EVALUATING YOUR PERFORMANCE

Now that you have scored your test, you may wish to compare your performance with the performance of others who took this test. Two kinds of information are provided, both using performance data from GRE Literature in English examinees tested between October 1986 and September 1989. Interpretive data based on the scores earned by examinees tested in this three-year period are to be used by admissions officers in 1990-91.

The first kind of information is based on the performance of a sample of the examinees who took the test in October 1989. This sample was selected to represent the total population of GRE Literature in English examinees tested between October 1986 and September 1989. On the work sheet you used to determine your score is a column labeled "P+." The numbers in this column indicate the percent of the examinees in this sample who answered each question correctly. You may use these numbers as a guide for evaluating your performance on each test question.

Also included, for each scaled score, is the percent of examinees tested between October 1986 and September 1989 who received lower scores. These percents appear in the score conversions table in a column to the right of the scaled scores. For example, in the percent column opposite the scaled score of 660 is the percent 91. This means that 91 percent of the Literature in English Test examinees tested between October 1986 and September 1989 scored lower than 660. To compare yourself with this population, look at the percent next to the scaled score you earned on the practice test. This number is a reasonable indication of your rank among GRE Literature in English Test examinees if you followed the test-taking suggestions in this practice book.

It is important to realize that the conditions under which you tested yourself were not exactly the same as those you will encounter at a test center. It is impossible to predict how different test-taking conditions will affect test performance, and this is only one factor that may account for differences between your practice test scores and your actual test scores. By comparing your performance on this practice test with the performance of other GRE Literature in English Test examinees, however, you will be able to determine your strengths and weaknesses and can then plan a program of study to prepare yourself for taking the Literature in English Test under standard conditions.

Before you start timing yourself on the test that follows, we suggest that you remove an answer sheet (pages 135 to 142) and turn first to the back cover of the test book (page 133), as you will do at the test center, and follow the instructions for completing the identification areas of the answer sheet. When you are ready to begin the test, note the time and start marking your answers to the questions on the answer sheet.

FORM GR9064
64

THE GRADUATE RECORD
EXAMINATIONS

LITERATURE IN ENGLISH TEST

*Do not break the seal
until you are told to do so.*

*The contents of this test are confidential.
Disclosure or reproduction of any portion
of it is prohibited.*

THIS TEST BOOK MUST NOT BE TAKEN FROM THE ROOM.

Copyright © 1989 by Educational Testing Service. All rights reserved.
Princeton, N.J. 08541

LITERATURE IN ENGLISH TEST

Time—170 minutes

230 Questions

Directions: Each of the questions or incomplete statements below is followed by five suggested answers or completions. Select the one that is best in each case and then completely fill in the corresponding oval on the answer sheet.

Questions 1-2

Slow wand'ring came the sightless sire and she,
Great-souled Antigone, the Grecian maid,
Leading with pace majestic his sad steps,
On whose bowed head grim Destiny had laid
A hand relentless.

1. The "sightless sire" (line 1) is

   (A) Priam
   (B) Paris
   (C) Oedipus
   (D) Orestes
   (E) Achilles

2. The usual grammatical pattern in which an adjective precedes the noun it modifies is inverted in lines

   (A) 1 and 2
   (B) 1 and 4
   (C) 2 and 4
   (D) 3 and 5
   (E) 4 and 5

3. 'Twere hard to say who fared the best:
      Sad mortals! thus the Gods still plague you!
   He lost his labour, I my jest:
      For he was drowned, and I've the ague.

   In the lines above, which Byron wrote after swimming the Hellespont, "he" refers to

   (A) Hercules
   (B) Abelard
   (C) Narcissus
   (D) Keats
   (E) Leander

GO ON TO THE NEXT PAGE.

Questions 4-6

> As toilsome I wander'd Virginia's woods,
> To the music of rustling leaves kick'd by my feet, (for 'twas autumn,)
> I mark'd at the foot of a tree the grave of a soldier;
> Mortally wounded he and buried on the retreat, (easily all I could understand,)
> (5) The halt of a mid-day hour, when up! no time to lose—yet this sign left,
> On a tablet scrawl'd and nail'd on the tree by the grave,
> *Bold, cautious, true, and my loving comrade.*

4. The "soldier" (line 3) died in the

   (A) Revolutionary War
   (B) War of 1812
   (C) Civil War
   (D) Spanish-American War
   (E) French and Indian Wars

5. Lines 4-7 contain

   (A) quotations from an official report documenting a military encounter
   (B) suppositions about the events and circumstances of the soldier's burial
   (C) prefigurations of the scene of the speaker's own death
   (D) a list of actual details of the retreat the speaker is recording
   (E) a retelling of a Biblical tale

6. The author of the lines is

   (A) Whitman
   (B) Emerson
   (C) Frost
   (D) Dickinson
   (E) Melville

GO ON TO THE NEXT PAGE.

Questions 7-9

The following imaginary sequence of remarks about the opening of Charles Dickens' *Great Expectations* takes place among critics of different theoretical persuasions.

7. Which speaker is a deconstructionist?

8. Which speaker is a Marxist?

9. Which speaker is a structuralist?

(A) Pip sets out here on the ambiguous quest which will define the novel itself and control its theme: the quest for identity. He seeks to find in his dead parents a clue to who he is but finds he must look beyond, particularly inside himself, to discover his true self. The irony is that at this beginning point there is nothing inside him. He is an empty vessel that the convict is about to start, most rudely, to fill.

(B) What humanist twaddle! The "self" you say he is searching for has nothing to do with the way the story forms itself. The story operates on a system of deep patterns common to most narratives, the most important of which is the contrast between the vertical and the horizontal. The Pip-agency is the "up" and his parents are the "down": soon Pip will be in a down position compared to the convict. One also notices in the opening scene a landscape which is horizontal. Pip, not a "character" but a factor, will move along both the horizontal and vertical axes in the book, a book which is not about quests and personality but *about* verticality and horizontality.

(C) All very stable and reassuring, isn't it, this boredom about the horizontal and the vertical; all very symmetrical, I'm sure. The difficulty is that you properly decenter the "human" and then, quite without warrant, center geometry. It's preposterous. There's no freeplay in your reading, no account of the way in which the self is set up as an empty signifier chasing after a signified it cannot find. "Pip" tries to inscribe himself in his parents' tombstone and finds himself being inscribed by forces about him. There is never a "self" in this story, as you say, but there isn't any "up" or "down" either; it is a totally decentered text, eluding any attempts to center or "understand" it.

(D) What I notice about all this talk is that it is anxious to put the "meaning" of your encounter with the text somewhere else. You are all so abstract, so quick to jump to larger patterns (or the absence of patterns), so spatializing. For me, the meaning is a process that is temporal, not spatial. Let's see: "My Father's family name" suggests a formal movement and a kind of deference that sets one up to respect the father and the power of the last name; I am guessing that the speaker is male . . ."being Pirrip" deflates the formal energy both by the grammar (this is not the main clause, I see) and by the odd, canary-like associations with "Pirrip"; "and my Christian name" . . .

(E) You divert yourselves with your talk about "process" and movement in time, when all along you completely ignore the historical content, the ideological forces at work here. You all are engaged in a flight from history into some universalist utopia! The opening shows an outcast from the machinery of social operation, a useless item trying desperately to recapture some position and some utility within the vicious and alienating mill of his culture.

GO ON TO THE NEXT PAGE.

10. It was on a dreary night of November, that I beheld the accomplishment of my toils. With an anxiety that almost amounted to agony, I collected the instruments of life around me, that I might infuse a spark of being into the lifeless thing that lay at my feet. . . . The rain pattered dismally against the panes, and my candle was nearly burnt out, when, by the glimmer of the half-extinguished light, I saw the dull yellow eye of the creature open; it breathed hard, and a convulsive motion agitated its limbs.

    The "I" of the passage above is

    (A) Mary Shelley's Frankenstein
    (B) Vladimir Nabokov's Kinbote
    (C) Nathaniel Hawthorne's Rappaccini
    (D) Herman Melville's Omoo
    (E) Edgar Allan Poe's Usher

11. Throughout its history, there has been a marked relation between the novel and the classical epic. Through the use of allusion, parody, stylistic imitation, or mythic parallels, that relation and its possibilities are exemplified by _____ in the eighteenth century and _____ in the twentieth.

    Which of the following will correctly complete the passage above?

    (A) Richardson's *Clarissa* . . . Woolf's *To the Lighthouse*
    (B) Sterne's *Tristram Shandy* . . . Lawrence's *Women in Love*
    (C) Smollett's *Humphry Clinker* . . . Faulkner's *Light in August*
    (D) Fielding's *Joseph Andrews* . . . Joyce's *Ulysses*
    (E) Fanny Burney's *Evelina* . . . Forster's *A Passage to India*

GO ON TO THE NEXT PAGE.

Questions 12-13

Major Arthur Barraclough, DSO, was the first to admit that the Army had gone to the dogs. You need look no further than a modern recruiting appeal to realise that. Composed by some long-haired PRO, who
(5) apparently had learned his craft in America, it read like a puff for a holiday camp. And the FDS, or Floosie Corps, as he ungallantly termed the women's sector, were a permanent thorn in his side.

But the Army had gone to the dogs in his father's
(10) day as well, when the famous crowd in which the Barracloughs served was combined, willy nilly, with a rabble of clots. It had done likewise in that of his grandfather, when the cavalry regiments were mechanized and commissions given to bounders. And the process had
(15) begun much earlier yet. The family archives were full of letters and diaries, musty and yellow, grieving over the milestones along the Army's downward path. There was the pampering initiated by Florence Nightingale, for instance, and the abolition of flogging. An entry in one
(20) journal, made on the eve of Waterloo, bemoaned the loss of fighting spirit among the rank and file; and a note in the margin by another hand, endorsing this, placed the turning-point at about the time of Malplaquet.
(25) It was a long melancholy saga of decline and decay.
....
....
A soldier was always a soldier, plenty of decent fellows were still joining up, and there were good little wars running somewhere most of the time.

12. The Major condemns modern recruiting appeals because they

   (A) promise to prepare recruits for vocations for which they are unsuited
   (B) address their efforts to upper-class recruits
   (C) fail to acknowledge the demands and rigors of Army life
   (D) stifle the initiative of senior officers like himself
   (E) ignore those who may be temperamentally unsuited to Army life

13. Which of the following is the sentence missing at lines 26-27 ?

   (A) Whenever he thought about it, he was moved to tears and anger, and he gave way to loud sobs.
   (B) If that was the way it was, he believed that there was no need to polish his medals and boots.
   (C) The Major was heartbroken and saddened, yet he consoled himself by hunting and farming.
   (D) Nevertheless, the Major said, there was no sense in whining at what was not to be helped.
   (E) Why, the Major wondered, did no one complain publicly about this state of affairs?

---

14. I am an American, Chicago born—Chicago, that somber city—and go at things as I have taught myself, free-style, and will make the record in my own way.

The speaker of the lines above is

   (A) Dreiser's Clyde Griffiths
   (B) Hemingway's Nick Adams
   (C) Melville's Ishmael
   (D) Fitzgerald's Dick Diver
   (E) Bellow's Augie March

GO ON TO THE NEXT PAGE.

Questions 15-17 refer to the excerpts below.

15. Which ends in an alexandrine?

16. Which is written in iambic tetrameter?

17. Which is written in imitation of Old English strong-stress verse?

(A) The witch that came (the withered hag)
To wash the steps with pail and rag
Was once the beauty Abishag.

(B) I stood in Venice, on the "Bridge of Sighs";
A Palace and a prison on each hand:
I saw from out the wave her structures rise
As from the stroke of the Enchanter's wand!
A thousand Years their cloudy wings expand
Around me, and a dying Glory smiles
O'er the far times, when many a subject land
Looked to the wingèd Lion's marble piles,
Where Venice sate in state, throned on her hundred isles!

(C) Wake all the dead! What ho-a! What ho-a!
How soundly they sleep whose pillows lie low;
They mind not poor lovers who walk above
On the decks of the world in storms of love.

(D) We set up mast and sail on that swart ship,
Bore sheep aboard her, and our bodies also
Heavy with weeping, and winds from sternward
Bore us on outward with bellying canvas,
Circe's this craft, the trim coifed goddess.

(E) As when upon a trancèd summer night,
Those green-robed senators of mighty woods,
Tall oaks, branch-charmèd by the earnest stars,
Dream, and so dream all night without a stir.

GO ON TO THE NEXT PAGE.

18. Let me give examples of how I began to develop the dim negative of Bigger. I met white writers who told me how whites reacted to this lurid American scene. And, as they talked I'd translate what they said in terms of Bigger's life. But what was more important still, I read their novels. Here, for the first time, I found ways and techniques of gauging meaningfully the effects of American civilization upon the personalities of people. I took these techniques, these ways of seeing and feeling, and twisted them, bent them, adapted them, until they became my ways of apprehending the locked-in life of the Black Belt areas.

    Which of the following accurately describes the passage above?

    (A) James Baldwin is discussing *Go Tell It on the Mountain*.
    (B) Maya Angelou is discussing *I Know Why the Caged Bird Sings*.
    (C) Ralph Ellison is discussing *Invisible Man*.
    (D) Zora Neale Hurston is discussing *Mules & Men*.
    (E) Richard Wright is discussing *Native Son*.

GO ON TO THE NEXT PAGE.

Questions 19-21 refer to the passages below.

19. In which is the "I" Moll Flanders?

20. In which is the "I" Pamela Andrews?

21. In which is the "I" Elizabeth Bennet?

(A) I lay in prison near fifteen weeks after this order for transportation was signed. What the reason of it was, I know not, but at the end of this time I was put on board of a ship in the Thames, and with me a gang of thirteen as hardened vile creatures as ever Newgate produced in my time.

(B) When I axed Mr. Clinker what they meant by calling me Issabel, he put the byebill into my hand, and I read of van Issabel a painted harlot, that vas thrown out of a vindore, and the dogs came and licked her blood—But I am no harlot; and, with God's blessing, no dog shall have my blood to lick: marry, Heaven forbid, amen!

(C) If there is no other objection to my marrying your nephew, I shall certainly not be kept from it, by knowing that his mother and aunt wished him to marry Miss De Bourgh. You both did as much as you could, in planning the marriage. Its completion depends on others. If Mr. Darcy is neither by honour nor inclination confined to his cousin, why is not he to make another choice?

(D) When I think of my danger, and the freedoms he actually took, I am almost distracted. I must leave off a little; for my eyes and my head are sadly bad. This was a dreadful trial! This was the worst of all! Oh! that I was out of the power of this dreadfully wicked man! Pray for your distressed daughter.

(E) If you don't come to me, I'll come to you, says he; I shan't come to you I assure you, says I. Upon which he run up, caught me in his Arms, and flung me upon a Chair, and began to offer to touch my Under-Petticoat. Sir, says I, you had better not offer to be rude; well, says he, no more I won't then; and away he went out of the Room. I was so mad to be sure I could have cry'd. Oh what a prodigious Vexation it is to a Woman to be made a Fool of.

GO ON TO THE NEXT PAGE.

Questions 22-23

Her sleeping head with its great gelid mass
   of serpents torpidly astir
burned into the mirroring shield—
   a scathing image, dire
(5) as hated truth the mind accepts at last
   and festers on.
I struck. The shield flashed bare.

Yet even as I lifted up the head
   and started from that place
(10) of gazing silences and terrored stone,
   I thirsted to destroy.
None could have passed me then—
   no garland-bearing girl, no priest
or staring boy—and lived.

"Perseus" is reprinted from *Angle of Ascent*, New and Selected Poems, by Robert Hayden, with the permission of Liveright Publishing Corporation. Copyright (c) 1975, 1972, 1970, 1966 by Robert Hayden.

22. Lines 1-2 describe

  (A) Clytemnestra
  (B) Medusa
  (C) Pandora
  (D) Venus
  (E) Andromache

23. Which of the following refers to "that place of gazing silences and terrored stone" (lines 9-10)?

  (A) As when the palsied universe aghast
     Lay . . . mute and still,
  When drove, so poets sing, the Sun-born youth
  Devious through Heaven's affrighted signs his sire's
  Ill-granted chariot. Him the Thunderer hurled
  From th' empyrean headlong to the gulf
  Of the half-parched Eridanus, where weep
  Even now the sister trees their amber tears.

  (B) In Xanadu did Kubla Khan
     A stately pleasure-dome decree,
  Where Alph, the sacred river, ran
  Through caverns measureless to man,
     Down to a sunless sea.

  (C) Driver of Phoebus' chariot, Phaeton,
  Struck by Jove's thunder, rests beneath this stone.
  He could not rule his father's car of fire,
    yet was it much so nobly to aspire.

  (D) But not in silence pass Calypso's isles,
  The sister tenants of the middle deep;
  There for the weary still a haven smiles,
  Though the fair goddess long has ceased to weep,
  And o'er her cliffs a fruitful watch to keep
  For him who dared prefer a mortal bride.

  (E) When wandering through the woods she turned to stone
  Their savage tenants; just as the foaming Lion
  Sprang furious on his prey, her speedier power
  Outran his haste,
  And fixed in that fierce attitude he stands
  Like Rage in marble!

GO ON TO THE NEXT PAGE.

24. A wealthy Venetian citizen, he is avariciousness incarnate. His greed and accompanying sensuality know no restraint; conscious of the same impulses in others, he works them—through his servant Mosca—to his own ends.

    The passage above discusses a leading character in

    (A) *The Rivals*
    (B) *Volpone*
    (C) *The Alchemist*
    (D) *The School for Scandal*
    (E) *Every Man in his Humour*

25. It is a chilling ghost story and an imaginative psychological study of a young governess confronted for the first time in her life with, at once, erotic infatuation, great responsibilities, the aftermath of human evil, and, she believes, the continued, haunting presence of that evil.

    The passage above describes

    (A) Conrad's *The Secret Sharer*
    (B) Fitzgerald's *Tender is the Night*
    (C) James's "The Turn of the Screw"
    (D) Poe's "The Purloined Letter"
    (E) O'Connor's *The Violent Bear It Away*

26. Dante's guide through the *Inferno* and *Purgatorio* is

    (A) Homer
    (B) Virgil
    (C) St. Paul
    (D) Boethius
    (E) Beatrice

Questions 27-29

The glories of our blood and state
Are shadows, not substantial things;
There is no armor against fate;
Death lays his icy hand on kings.
(5) Scepter and crown
Must tumble down,
And in the dust be equal made
With the poor crooked scythe and spade.

27. The closest synonym for "blood" (line 1) is

    (A) lineage
    (B) strife
    (C) suffering
    (D) sacrifice
    (E) hopefulness

28. Lines 5-8 provide examples of

    (A) oxymoron
    (B) metonymy
    (C) simile
    (D) hyperbole
    (E) synaesthesia

29. Which of the following is the best summary of the theme of the passage?

    (A) Uneasy lies the head that wears a crown.
    (B) Death is the mother of beauty.
    (C) Pride goeth before a fall.
    (D) Death is the great leveller.
    (E) My mind to me a kingdom is.

GO ON TO THE NEXT PAGE.

30. The heroine of the novel, an innocent peasant girl, is the victim not only of her Victorian environment but also of people, including her shiftless parents, her cruel seducer, and her morally rigid husband, Angel Clare, who recognizes too late his wife's fundamental purity.

    The passage above describes

    (A) Richardson's *Clarissa*
    (B) Austen's *Emma*
    (C) Brontë's *Jane Eyre*
    (D) Eliot's *Silas Marner*
    (E) Hardy's *Tess of the D'Urbervilles*

Questions 31-32

Do you feel thankful, ay or no,
For this fair town's face, yonder river's line,
The mountain round it and the sky above,
Much more the figures of man, woman, child,
(5) These are the frame to? What's it all about?
To be passed over, despised? or dwelt upon,
Wondered at? oh, this last of course!—you say.
But why not do as well as say, paint these
Just as they are, careless what comes of it?
(10) God's works—paint any one, and count it crime
To let a truth slip. Don't object, "His works
Are here already; nature is complete;
Suppose you reproduce her (which you can't)
There's no advantage! you must beat her, then."
(15) For, don't you mark? we're made so that we love
First when we see them painted, things we have passed
Perhaps a hundred times nor cared to see;
And so they are better, painted—better to us,
Which is the same thing. Art was given for that;
(20) God uses us to help each other so,
Lending our minds out.

31. In context, "To let a truth slip" (line 11) means to

    (A) reveal a truth inadvertently
    (B) presume to improve upon Nature
    (C) disobey God's commandments
    (D) fail to paint each detail accurately
    (E) fail to follow the prescribed rules for art

32. The theory of art advanced by the speaker in his conclusion (lines 15-21) holds that art

    (A) represents generalities, not particulars
    (B) fosters affection for what it represents
    (C) is wholly separate from the moral life of the observer
    (D) restores us to mental health by purging troublesome emotions
    (E) advances through a transformation of the ideas of predecessors

GO ON TO THE NEXT PAGE.

Questions 33-34

I was unlike others of my generation in one thing only. I am very religious, and deprived by Huxley and Tyndall, whom I detested, of the simple-minded religion of my childhood, I had made a new religion, almost an
(5) infallible church of poetic tradition, of a fardel of stories, and of personages, and of emotions, inseparable from their first expression, passed on from generation to generation by poets and painters with some help from philosophers and theologians. I wished for a world
(10) where I could discover this tradition perpetually, and not in pictures and in poems only, but in tiles round the chimney-piece and in the hangings that kept out the draft.

33. In the context of the passage, "Huxley and Tyndall" (lines 2-3) are meant to stand for

(A) Victorian scientific naturalism
(B) socialist agitation
(C) the confusion of religion and art
(D) liberal morality
(E) conservative religious reaction

34. In wishing "for a world where I could discover this tradition perpetually" (lines 9-10), the speaker is asking for a world where

(A) traditional crafts would be replaced by modern art
(B) artistic endeavors would be amply rewarded
(C) the tradition would permeate all aspects of life
(D) scholars would be freed from all practical concerns
(E) the performance of religious duties would supersede all other activities

35. The German novelist Christa Wolf has observed that the most likely female hero for the modern woman's *Iliad* is _____. She alone of Priam's daughters preferred not to marry. A priestess of Apollo, she had from him the gift of true prophecy, though no one was willing to believe what she said.

Which of the following will correctly complete line 2 ?

(A) Leda
(B) Helen
(C) Medea
(D) Cassandra
(E) Jocasta

GO ON TO THE NEXT PAGE.

Questions 36-38 refer to the excerpts below.

36. Which alludes to a poem by Marvell?

37. Which alludes to a poem by Marlowe?

38. Which alludes to a poem by Herrick?

(A) Whenas galoshed my Julia goes,
    Unbuckled all from top to toes,
    How swift the poem becometh prose!

(B) Time's Wingéd Chariot (poets say)
    Warns us to love while yet we may;
    Must I not hurry all the more
    Who find it parked outside my door?

(C) "Come live with me and be my love"
        He said, in substance. "There's no vine
    We will not pluck the clusters of,
        Or grape we will not turn to wine."

(D) More luck to honest poverty,
        It claims respect, and a' that;
    But honest wealth's a better thing,
        We dare be rich for a' that.

(E) He lived amidst th' untrodden ways
        To Rydal Lake that lead;
    A bard whom there were none to praise,
        And very few to read.

GO ON TO THE NEXT PAGE.

39. The tragedy of Phaedra and her love for her stepson has been dramatized by

    (A) Aeschylus and Shakespeare
    (B) Ionesco and Pinter
    (C) Goethe and Schiller
    (D) Chekhov and Ibsen
    (E) Euripides and Racine

40. Ðā wæs æfter manigum dagum, ðæt sē cyning cōm tō ðām ēalande.

    Which of the following is the best rendering of the Old English line above?

    (A) Yes, it was so that afterward many dogs and swans returned to them on the landing.
    (B) See the king come to the dam on the island that was dry during the flood.
    (C) Then it was after many days that the king came to the island.
    (D) There was pursuing this magnificent dog a king come to search for him.
    (E) Only after ten men were captured with many daggers did the cunning soldiers come to land.

Questions 41-43

    To "Lydia Languish"

You ask me, Lydia, "whether I,
If you refuse my suit, shall die."
    (Now pray don't let this hurt you!)
Although the time be out of joint,
(5) I should not think a bodkin's point
    The sole resource of virtue;
Nor shall I, though your mood endure,
Attempt a final Water-cure
    Except against my wishes;
(10) For I respectfully decline
To dignify the Serpentine,
    And make *hors-d'oeuvres* for fishes;
But if you ask me whether I
    Composedly can go,
(15) Without a look, without a sigh,
    Why, then I answer—No.

41. The speaker in the poem suggests to "Lydia" that he

    (A) will gladly die for her
    (B) cannot abide her coyness any longer
    (C) will curse his fate upon her leaving
    (D) will not be unfaithful to her
    (E) will do nothing melodramatic if she refuses him

42. Lines 4-5 allude to

    (A) *Hamlet*
    (B) *Othello*
    (C) *Macbeth*
    (D) *King Lear*
    (E) *Antony and Cleopatra*

43. "To dignify the Serpentine" (line 11) means

    (A) to pay homage to Medusa
    (B) to trust women
    (C) to visit brothels
    (D) to drown oneself
    (E) to fish

GO ON TO THE NEXT PAGE.

44. The king of this land looks upon Gulliver's kind as "diminutive insects"; after learning about English society, he concludes that the English are "the most pernicious race of little odious vermin that nature ever suffered to crawl upon the surface of the earth."

The king described above rules

(A) Houyhnhnmland
(B) Lilliput
(C) Laputa
(D) Brobdingnag
(E) Glubdubdrib

45. When the stars threw down their spears,
     And water'd heaven with their tears,
     Did he smile his work to see?
     Did he who made the Lamb make thee?

The "thee" addressed in the lines above is

(A) a waterfowl
(B) a tiger
(C) a man
(D) a woman
(E) the reader

Questions 46-47

Travelling is a fool's paradise. Our first journeys discover to us the indifference of places. At home I dream that at Naples, at Rome, I can be intoxicated with beauty, and lose my sadness. I pack my trunk, (5) embrace my friends, embark on the sea and at last wake up in Naples, and there beside me is the stern fact, the sad self, unrelenting, identical, that I fled from. I seek the Vatican, and the palaces. I affect to be intoxicated with sights and suggestions but I am not intoxicated. My giant goes with me wherever I go.

46. In context, the second sentence of the paragraph means that on our first journeys we discover that

(A) foreigners are unconcerned about our welfare
(B) it really does not matter where we are
(C) no place lacks charms of some sort
(D) the most exciting part of any trip is the journey home
(E) the most recent place we have been always compares unfavorably with the place in which we now find ourselves

47. In line 8, "I affect to be" is best paraphrased as

(A) I consider myself
(B) I discourse on being
(C) I question whether I am
(D) I cannot be said to be
(E) I pretend to be

GO ON TO THE NEXT PAGE.

Questions 48-49

Transcendental truth comes in experiential blobs rather than in systems of knowledge, as one critic has reported, having been one of the very few blessed with the gift of untranslatable epiphanies or visionary gleams. Tranquilly recollecting such blobs of time, he can afford to abandon all connected forms of culture from chronology to logic while he crawls back into the shell of Romantic individualism.

48. In which of the following does the author allude to specific phrases from the writings of Wordsworth?

    (A) "Transcendental truth," "experiential blobs," "systems of knowledge"
    (B) "the very few," "blessed with the gift," "untranslatable epiphanies"
    (C) "visionary gleams," "Tranquilly recollecting," "blobs of time"
    (D) "afford to abandon," "connected forms of culture," "chronology to logic"
    (E) "crawls back," "into the shell," "Romantic individualism"

49. The author suggests that the critic under consideration

    (A) bases his ideas on common human experience
    (B) grasps truth beyond the understanding of most critics
    (C) possesses an extraordinary memory
    (D) provides intuitions rather than reasoned arguments
    (E) prefers visionary gleams to Romantic individualism

---

50. Though best known as a poet, _____ wrote a series of stories about Simple, a street-smart, amused and amusing, sad and scarred—though never less than resilient and irrepressible—resident of Harlem.

    The author whose name will correctly complete line 1 is

    (A) Langston Hughes
    (B) James Dickey
    (C) Amiri Baraka
    (D) John Ashbery
    (E) Claude McKay

Questions 51-52

Oh, weep for Adonais—he is dead!
Wake, melancholy Mother, wake and weep!
Yet wherefore? Quench within their burning bed
Thy fiery tears, and let thy loud heart keep
Like his, a mute and uncomplaining sleep;
For he is gone, where all things wise and fair
Descend—oh, dream not that the amorous Deep
Will yet restore him to the vital air;
Death feeds on his mute voice, and laughs at our despair.

51. The stanza is from an elegy for

    (A) Wordsworth
    (B) Byron
    (C) Blake
    (D) Keats
    (E) Coleridge

52. The form of the stanza is that of

    (A) ottava rima
    (B) rhyme royal
    (C) terza rima
    (D) the "In Memoriam" stanza
    (E) the Spenserian stanza

GO ON TO THE NEXT PAGE.

53. You see, I had a design in my mind. I had a design. To accomplish it I should require money, a house, a plantation, slaves, a family—incidentally, of course, a wife. I set out to acquire these, asking no favor of any man.

    The "I" of the lines above is

    (A) Starbuck in *Moby Dick*
    (B) Colonel Thomas Sutpen in *Absalom, Absalom!*
    (C) Jake Barnes in *The Sun Also Rises*
    (D) Lambert Strether in *The Ambassadors*
    (E) Clifford Pyncheon in *The House of the Seven Gables*

Questions 54-55

Here was _____, in the year 1621, unanimously chosen the governor of the plantation: the difficulties whereof were such, that if he had not been a person of more than ordinary piety, wisdom and courage, he must have sunk under them. He had, with a laudable industry, been laying up a treasure of experiences, and he had now occasion to use it: indeed, nothing but an *experienced* man could have been suitable to the necessities of the people.

54. The individual "unanimously chosen" governor was

    (A) William Bradford
    (B) William Byrd
    (C) Edward Taylor
    (D) Jonathan Edwards
    (E) Cotton Mather

55. The "plantation" referred to in the passage was

    (A) Jamestown
    (B) Salem
    (C) Plymouth
    (D) Charleston
    (E) Philadelphia

GO ON TO THE NEXT PAGE.

Questions 56-57

>Luckes, my faire falcon, and your fellowes all,
>How wel pleasaunt yt were your libertie!
>Ye do not forsake me that faire might ye befall.
>But they that somtyme lykt my companye
>*(5)* Lyke lyse awaye from ded bodies thei crall:
>Loe what a profe in light adversytie!
>But ye my birdes, I swear by all your belles,
>Ye be my fryndes, and so be but few elles.

56. Which of the following accurately describes the lines?

   (A) The speaker contrasts the behavior of his falcon and the behavior of his sometime friends.
   (B) The speaker recalls the pleasant freedom and vigor of his youth when he caroused noisily with his friends.
   (C) The speaker knows that death is near and wishes to be a bird so that he can fly from scenes of death.
   (D) The speaker praises his lover for not forsaking him.
   (E) The speaker recounts his fond memories of a youth spent in hunting and lovemaking.

57. The poem was written about the year

   (A) 800
   (B) 1030
   (C) 1250
   (D) 1530
   (E) 1720

Questions 58-59

>It afforded Mr. Bounderby supreme satisfaction to install himself in this snug little estate, and with demonstrative humility to grow cabbages in the flower-garden. He delighted to live, barrack-fashion, among the elegant furniture, and he bullied the very pictures with his origin. "Why, Sir," he would say to a visitor, "I am told that Nickits," the late owner, "gave seven hundred pounds for that Seabeach. Now, to be plain with you, if I ever, in the whole course of my life, take seven looks at it, at a hundred pounds a look, it will be as much as I shall do. No, by George! I don't forget that I am Josiah Bounderby of Coketown."

58. The passage depicts Bounderby as

   (A) a simple farmer who is overawed by the surroundings in which he finds himself
   (B) a cantankerous sea captain who is forced to sell off his valuable property
   (C) a retired army officer who longs for the pomp and ceremony of the military life
   (D) an aristocrat who has become bored with his elegant possessions
   (E) a prosperous man who delights in feigning contempt for the signs of his wealth

59. The passage is from

   (A) *The Mayor of Casterbridge*
   (B) *Emma*
   (C) *Hard Times*
   (D) *Tom Jones*
   (E) *Adam Bede*

GO ON TO THE NEXT PAGE.

Questions 60-63 refer to the passages below.

60. Which is written by a psychoanalytical critic?

61. Which discusses Othello in terms of the Faustian myth?

62. In which of the passages is the critic applying the neoclassical rules of decorum?

63. In which passage is the critic's method based on the study of recurrent image patterns?

(A) Nothing is more odious in Nature than an improbable lye; And, certainly, never was any Play fraught, like this of *Othello*, with improbabilities. The Characters or Manners, which are the second part in a Tragedy, are not less unnatural and improper, than the Fable was improbable and absurd....

But what is most intolerable is Iago. He is no Black-amoor Souldier, so we may be sure he should be like other Souldiers of our acquaintance; yet never in Tragedy, nor in Comedy, nor in Nature was a Souldier with his Character.... but to entertain the Audience with something new and surprising, against common sense, and Nature, he would pass upon a close, dissembling, false, insinuating rascal, instead of an open-hearted, frank, plain-dealing Souldier, a character constantly worn by them for some thousands of years in the World.

(B) The moment of his kneeling to vow revenge is the moment of Othello's giving himself over to Iago. "Do not rise yet," commands Iago.... He kneels side by side with Othello and vows to be at his service in "what bloody business ever." The oaths that the two exchange are horrifying in their solemnity: it is a pact with the devil Othello has made. "Now art thou my lieutenant," says Othello. "I am your own for ever," replies Iago in the last words of the scene. Iago becomes Othello's Mephistopheles, and in making the devil his servant Othello gives himself up into his power.

(C) *Othello* ... is pure melodrama. There is not a touch of character in it that goes below the skin; and the fitful attempts to make Iago something better than a melodramatic villain only make a hopeless mess of him and his motives. To anyone capable of reading the play with an open mind as to its merits, it is obvious that Shakespeare plunged through it so impetuously that he had finished before he had made up his mind as to the character and motives of a single person in it. Probably it was not until he stumbled into the sentimental fit in which he introduced the willow song that he saw his way through without making Desdemona enough of the "supersubtle Venetian" of Iago's description to strengthen the case for Othello's jealousy.

(D) The sudden onset of Iago's disturbance is most comparable to a state of panic. He tries at first to rationalize his excitement. He insists that his jealousy is caused only by his failure to attain the post he desired and by its having been conferred on Cassio instead. However, the basic conflict is revealed in Iago's choice of words: "Preferment goes by letter and affection, and not by old gradation" (I.i.36-37). The words "preferment" and "affection" point up the fact that Iago's hurt stems not only from a blow to professional pride, but from a rupture in his love relationship—another has been taken into favor in his stead.

(E) Throughout *Othello* we are reminded of animals in action, preying upon one another, mischievous, lascivious, cruel, or suffering, and through these, the general sense of pain and unpleasantness is much increased and kept constantly before us.

More than half the references to animals in the play are Iago's, and all these are contemptuous or repellent, a plague of flies, a quarrelsome dog, bird-snaring, leading asses by the nose, a spider catching a fly, beating an offenceless dog, wild cats, wolves, goats, and monkeys.

GO ON TO THE NEXT PAGE.

64. Weele lead you to the stately tent of War,
    Where you shall heare the Scythian _____
    Threatning the world with high astounding tearms
    And scourging kingdoms with his conquering sword.

    Which of the following will correctly complete line 2 ?

    (A) Faustus
    (B) Volpone
    (C) Malvolio
    (D) Tamburlaine
    (E) Oedipus

65. Identifying the audience for all her writing as "a people who think God is dead," she has dramatized the theological insight behind Francis Thompson's "Hound of Heaven": God pursues us until we finally discover that everything we seek can be found only in Him. The pursued in *Wise Blood* is Hazel Motes, a young Army veteran who is obsessed with the idea of starting a church without Christ. Claiming that "all my stories are about the action of grace on a character who is not very willing to support it," the author described *Wise Blood* as "a comic novel about a Christian *malgré lui*." Every time Hazel rails against God and proclaims His absence from the world, God's presence is comically but undeniably reintroduced.

    The passage above discusses the work of

    (A) Flannery O'Connor
    (B) Eudora Welty
    (C) Edith Wharton
    (D) Iris Murdoch
    (E) Doris Lessing

GO ON TO THE NEXT PAGE.

Questions 66-70

Darknesse and light divide the course of time, and oblivion shares with memory, a great part even of our living beings; we slightly remember our felicities, and the smartest stroaks of affliction leave but short smart upon
(5) us. Sense endureth no extremities, and sorrows destroy us or themselves. To weep into stones are fables. Afflictions induce callosities, miseries are slippery, or fall like snow upon us, which notwithstanding is no unhappy stupidity. To be ignorant of evils to come, and forgetful
(10) of evils past, is a mercifull provision in nature, whereby we digest the mixture of our few and evil dayes, and our delivered senses not relapsing into cutting remembrances, our sorrows are not kept raw by the edge of repetitions. A great part of Antiquity contented their
(15) hopes of subsistency with a transmigration of their souls. A good way to continue their memories, while having the advantage of plurall successions, they could not but act something remarkable in such variety of beings, and enjoying the fame of their passed selves, make accumula-
(20) tion of glory unto their last durations. Others rather then be lost in the uncomfortable night of nothing, were content to recede into the common being, and make one particle of the publick soul of all things, which was no more then to return into their unknown and divine Orig-
(25) inall again. Egyptian ingenuity was more unsatisfied, contriving their bodies in sweet consistences, to attend the return of their souls. But all was vanity, feeding the winde, and folly. The Egyptian Mummies, which Cambyses or time hath spared, avarice now consumeth.
(30) Mummie is become Merchandise, Mizraim cures wounds, and Pharaoh is sold for balsoms.

66. The closest synonym for "oblivion" (line 2) is

 (A) destruction
 (B) forgetfulness
 (C) ignorance
 (D) neglect
 (E) invective

67. Which of the following is the closest restatement of "Sense endureth no extremities, and sorrows destroy us or themselves" (lines 5-6)?

 (A) Intense pain either kills the sufferer or by its very intensity dulls the perception of it.
 (B) An intelligent person avoids extreme danger and thereby lessens the chance of perishing.
 (C) A hand or foot numbed by pain is likely to be further injured and may cause the death of its owner.
 (D) Only if we refuse to give way completely to great grief can we avoid the possibility of succumbing to it.
 (E) Rightly considered, sense impressions are fleeting representations of reality, and so feelings of sadness should be totally ignored.

68. The myth alluded to in line 6 ("weep into stones") is a story about

 (A) Tantalus
 (B) Prometheus
 (C) Niobe
 (D) Midas
 (E) Pandora

69. Which of the following best describes the tone of the passage?

 (A) At the beginning it is harshly admonitory, but it gradually changes into superciliousness.
 (B) It moves from invective at the beginning to objective description and then culminates in impassioned pleading.
 (C) It is essentially detached and scientific, but with undertones of disdain and condescension.
 (D) It moves almost imperceptibly from tongue-in-cheek epigram to outright burlesque.
 (E) It begins aphoristically, becomes more discursive, and then concludes with a satirical epigram.

70. The groups of ancients discussed in lines 14-31 are all used as examples of

 (A) misguided pagan materialism
 (B) attempts to confront the apparent finality of death
 (C) the superiority of the accomplishments of ancient philosophy
 (D) means of revering historical remains
 (E) forerunners of monotheistic religion

GO ON TO THE NEXT PAGE.

Questions 71-77. For each of the following passages, identify the author or the work. Base your decision on the content and style of each passage.

71. If you are lucky enough to have lived in Paris as a young man, then wherever you go for the rest of your life, it stays with you, for Paris is a moveable feast.

    (A) T. S. Eliot
    (B) Stevens
    (C) Bellow
    (D) Hemingway
    (E) Poe

72. I lived on the plantation of Col. Lloyd, on the eastern shore of Maryland, and belonged to that gentleman's clerk. He owned, probably, not less than a thousand slaves. I mention the name of this man, and also of the persons who perpetrated the deeds which I am about to relate, running the risk of being hurled back into interminable bondage—for I am yet a slave;—yet for the sake of the cause—for the sake of humanity, I will mention the names, and glory in running the risk.

    (A) Frederick Douglass
    (B) Booker T. Washington
    (C) Richard Wright
    (D) Phillis Wheatley
    (E) W.E.B. Du Bois

73.
>   Among the rain
>   and lights
>   I saw the figure 5
>   in gold
>   on a red
>   firetruck
>   moving
>   tense
>   unheeded
>   to gong clangs
>   siren howls
>   and wheels rumbling
>   through the dark city.

    Copyright © 1938 by New Directions Publishing Corporation. Reprinted by permission of New Directions Publishing Corporation.

    (A) Ezra Pound
    (B) Emily Dickinson
    (C) Robert Frost
    (D) William Carlos Williams
    (E) Robert Lowell

74. Our novelists . . . concern themselves with the more smiling aspects of life, which are the more American . . . . It is worthwhile, even at the risk of being called common-place, to be true to our well-to-do actualities; the very passions themselves seem to be softened and modified by conditions which formerly at least could not be said to wrong any one, to cramp endeavor, or to cross lawful desire.

    (A) Howells
    (B) Twain
    (C) Hawthorne
    (D) Emerson
    (E) Melville

75. Well that was yesterday and to-day is the landing and we heard Eisenhower tell us he was here they were here and just yesterday a man sold us ten packages of Camel cigarettes, glory be, and we are singing glory hallelujah, and feeling very nicely, and everybody has been telephoning to us congratulatory messages upon my birthday which it isn't but we know what they mean.

    (A) Sylvia Plath
    (B) Gertrude Stein
    (C) Katherine Anne Porter
    (D) William Faulkner
    (E) James Joyce

76. The way to the Celestial City lies just through this town, where the lusty fair is kept; and he that will go to the City, and yet not go through this town, must needs go out of the world.

    (A) Bunyan's *The Pilgrim's Progress*
    (B) Thoreau's *Walden*
    (C) Swift's *Gulliver's Travels*
    (D) Hawthorne's *The Scarlet Letter*
    (E) Defoe's *Roxana*

77. I say that a cultivated intellect, because it is a good in itself, brings with it a power and a grace to every work and occupation which it undertakes, and enables us to be more useful, and to a greater number. There is a duty we owe to human society as such, to the state to which we belong, to the sphere in which we move, to the individuals towards whom we are variously related, and whom we successively encounter in life; and that philosophical or liberal education, as I have called it, which is the proper function of a University, if it refuses the foremost place to professional interests, does but postpone them to the formation of the citizen.

    (A) Carlyle
    (B) Ruskin
    (C) Newman
    (D) Morris
    (E) Wilde

GO ON TO THE NEXT PAGE.

78. At home is naught but making love to every painted post.
    Abroade the flesh is tamde, and brought in feare and frame,
    At home oft times pride goes before, and after commeth shame.
    Abroade we wisedome learne, and do from follie flee;
    At home some daunce so in a nette theirselves they cannot see.
    Abroade where service is, much honour may be wonne;
    At home our gay vayne-glory goes like shadow in the sunne.

    The lines above contrast "home" and "abroade"; home is seen as a place of

    (A) independence and health, abroad as a place of servitude and dependency
    (B) nobility and virtue, abroad as a place of greed and sophistication
    (C) learning and sorrow, abroad as a place of hardship and disease
    (D) warmth and loving kindness, abroad as a place of vice and despair
    (E) dissipation and immorality, abroad as a place of industry and abstemiousness

GO ON TO THE NEXT PAGE.

Questions 79-82

Much he the place admired, the person more.
As one who long in populous city pent,
Where houses thick and sewers annoy the air,
Forth issuing on a summer's morn to breathe
(5) Among the pleasant villages and farms
Adjoined, from each thing met conceives delight,
The smell of grain, or tedded grass, or kine,
Or dairy, each rural sight, each rural sound;
If chance with nymph-like step fair virgin pass,
(10) What pleasing seemed, for her now pleases more,
She most, and in her look sums all delight.
Such pleasure took the serpent to behold
This flowery plat, the sweet recess of Eve
Thus early, thus alone.

79. The subject of "conceives" (line 6) is

(A) "one" (line 2)
(B) "villages and farms" (line 5)
(C) "each" (line 6)
(D) "chance" (line 9)
(E) "virgin" (line 9)

80. Which of the following is closest in meaning to "for" in line 10 ?

(A) in spite of
(B) so that
(C) belonging to
(D) except for
(E) because of

81. Which of the conventions of the epic is illustrated in the passage?

(A) The epic simile
(B) The perilous journey
(C) The epic invocation
(D) The intervention of the gods
(E) The beginning *in medias res*

82. Which of the following passages also appears in the poem?

(A) Dry clashed his harness in the icy caves
And barren chasms, and all to left and right
The bare black cliff clanged round him, as he based
His feet on juts of slippery crag that rang
Sharp-smitten with the dint of armed heels—
And on a sudden, lo! the level lake,
And the long glories of the winter moon.

(B) In squandering wealth was his peculiar art:
Nothing went unrewarded, but desert.
Beggar'd by fools, whom still he found too late:
He had his jest, and they had his estate.

(C) Of Man's first disobedience, and the fruit
Of that forbidden tree, whose mortal taste
Brought death into the World, and all our woe,
With loss of Eden, till one greater Man
Restore us, and regain the blissful seat,
Sing, Heavenly Muse.

(D) All nature is but art unknown to thee,
All chance, direction which thou canst not see;
All discord, harmony not understood;
All partial evil, universal good;
And, spite of pride, in erring reason's spite,
One truth is clear: Whatever is, is right.

(E) That is no country for old men. The young
In one another's arms, birds in the trees
—Those dying generations—at their song,
The salmon-falls, the mackerel-crowded seas,
Fish, flesh, or fowl, commend all summer long
Whatever is begotten, born and dies,
Caught in that sensual music all neglect
Monuments of unageing intellect.

GO ON TO THE NEXT PAGE.

83.
```
              within the hollow crown
That rounds the mortal temples of a king
Keeps Death his court; and there the antic sits,
Scoffing his state and grinning at his pomp;
Allowing him a breath, a little scene,
To monarchize, be fear'd, and kill with looks.
```

Which of the following is the best summary of the lines from *Richard II* above?

(A) Life, not death, reveals the flaws of even the most powerful kings.
(B) Kings use death to maintain their pomp and power.
(C) The absolute power of a king permits him to scoff at death because he is secure in the knowledge of his place in history.
(D) The ever-present reality of death makes a king's royal state and power a kind of ironic show.
(E) Because a king can scoff at death, he rules as if there were no threat to his power, authority, or person.

Questions 84-87 refer to the openings of the novels below.

84. Which begins *Candide*?

85. Which begins *Anna Karenina*?

86. Which begins *Crime and Punishment*?

87. Which begins García Márquez' *One Hundred Years of Solitude*?

(A) We were in class when the headmaster came in, followed by a new boy not wearing the school uniform, and a school servant carrying a large desk. Those who had been asleep woke up, and everyone rose as if just surprised at his work.

(B) Happy families are all alike; every unhappy family is unhappy in its own way.

(C) Many years later, as he faced the firing squad, Colonel Aureliano Buendía was to remember that distant afternoon when his father took him to discover ice.

(D) There lived in Westphalia, at the country seat of Baron Thunder-ten-tronckh, a young lad blessed by nature with the most agreeable manners. You could read his character in his face. He combined sound judgment with unaffected simplicity.

(E) Towards the end of a sultry afternoon early in July a young man came out of his little room in Stolyarny Lane and turned slowly and somewhat irresolutely in the direction of Kamenny Bridge.

GO ON TO THE NEXT PAGE.

88. It can be argued that these protagonists are the Ur-figures of American fiction. Both are men obsessed with an idea of godliness and personal purity. Both pursue the idea in the conquest of, or escape into, undefiled nature. One is overtaken and finally destroyed by the evils of civilization he was presumptuous and innocent enough to flee, while the other presumes beyond the limits of human power and is defeated by a force that is natural and cosmic.

    The passage above discusses

    (A) Dimmesdale and Lambert Strether
    (B) Huck Finn and Tom Sawyer
    (C) Joe Christmas and Flem Snopes
    (D) Leatherstocking and Captain Ahab
    (E) Gatsby and Nick Carraway

89. Similar in theme and situation to Dryden's *Mac Flecknoe*, in which an inferior poet is named ruler of the Kingdom of Nonsense, this poem satirizes a legion of inferior poets and critics who worship the Goddess Dullness, daughter of Chaos and Night, and her Princes—Lewis Theobald and Colley Cibber.

    The poem described above is

    (A) *Hudibras*
    (B) *The Rape of the Lock*
    (C) *The Vanity of Human Wishes*
    (D) *The Dunciad*
    (E) *Absalom and Achitophel*

90. Despite his accomplishments and honors, the protagonist is overcome by the beauty of a Polish boy and, obsessed by love, dies of the plague in Venice.

    The passage above describes

    (A) Mann's Gustav von Aschenbach
    (B) Tolstoi's Count Vronsky
    (C) Proust's Swann
    (D) Stendhal's Julien Sorel
    (E) Balzac's Goriot

Questions 91-93

"I lived my life out to the very end
And passed the stages Fortune had appointed.
Now my tall shade goes to the under world.
I built a famous town, saw my great walls,
(5) Avenged my husband, made my hostile brother
Pay for his crime. Happy, alas, too happy,
If only the Dardanian keels had never
Beached on our coast." And here she kissed the bed.
"I die unavenged," she said, "but let me die.
(10) This way, this way, a blessed relief to go
Into the undergloom. Let the cold Trojan,
Far at sea, drink in this conflagration
And take with him the omen of my death!"

91. The "famous town" (line 4) is

    (A) Camelot
    (B) Sparta
    (C) Carthage
    (D) Athens
    (E) Pompeii

92. The "cold Trojan" (line 11) is

    (A) Ulysses
    (B) Aeneas
    (C) Hector
    (D) Priam
    (E) Agamemnon

93. These lines are spoken as

    (A) Antigone addresses Creon
    (B) Clytemnestra prepares to receive her son
    (C) Medea prepares to murder her children
    (D) Electra greets Orestes
    (E) Dido commits suicide

GO ON TO THE NEXT PAGE.

94. The play is lurid and complicated. There is the heroine's secret and forbidden marriage to her steward Antonio. There are her two evil brothers: Ferdinand, who is driven mad by incestuous passion for her, and the Cardinal, who has schemed to be Pope. After her marriage is discovered, she is imprisoned and tormented. At the end, everyone dies violently.

    The passage above describes

    (A) Kyd's *The Spanish Tragedy*
    (B) Jonson's *Volpone*
    (C) Goldsmith's *She Stoops to Conquer*
    (D) Sheridan's *The Rivals*
    (E) Webster's *The Duchess of Malfi*

Questions 95-98

Dame Caelia men did her call, as thought
　From Heaven to come, or thither to arise,
　The mother of three daughters, well upbrought
　In goodly thewes, and godly exercise:
(5) The eldest two most sober, chast, and wise,
　Fidelia and Speranza virgins were,
　Though spousd, yet wanting wedlocks solemnize;
　But faire Charissa to a lovely fere*
Was linckéd, and by him had many pledges dere.

*mate

95. The "three daughters" (line 3) are

    (A) Hera, Athena, and Aphrodite
    (B) the Three Fates
    (C) the Muses of Dance, History, and Comedy
    (D) the Three Graces
    (E) Faith, Hope, and Charity

96. The closest synonym for "wanting" (line 7) is

    (A) desiring
    (B) demanding
    (C) hindering
    (D) lacking
    (E) preventing

97. In context, the phrase "pledges dere" (line 9) refers to

    (A) broken promises
    (B) unwelcome presents
    (C) beloved children
    (D) a meager dowry
    (E) dour smiles

98. The stanza appears in

    (A) *Beowulf*
    (B) *The Faerie Queene*
    (C) *Paradise Lost*
    (D) *Childe Harold's Pilgrimage*
    (E) *Hyperion*

GO ON TO THE NEXT PAGE.

99. What spoke to Mrs. Moore in the nothingness of the cave was something ancient, "the undying worm itself," the echo that coils around the walls, denying value to "poor little talkative Christianity" and reason alike, so levelling everything that discriminations are impossible.

    The passage above is from a discussion of

    (A) Forster's *A Passage to India*
    (B) James's *The Golden Bowl*
    (C) Murdoch's *A Severed Head*
    (D) Joyce's *Ulysses*
    (E) Lawrence's *The Rainbow*

100. The novel begins one fine morning with the arrest of Joseph K., a respectable functionary in a bank, and ends with his execution almost 300 pages later, with neither the victim nor the reader any closer to an understanding of his "crime." What is most disturbing is not so much that Joseph K. died "like a dog" after an executioner plunged a knife into his heart, but that he was sentenced to death for no apparent reason.

    The novel discussed above is

    (A) Orwell's *1984*
    (B) Pynchon's *Gravity's Rainbow*
    (C) Bellow's *Dangling Man*
    (D) Kafka's *The Trial*
    (E) Hemingway's *A Farewell to Arms*

101. Do not forever with thy veiled lids
    Seek for thy noble father in the dust:
    Thou know'st 'tis common; all that lives must die
    Passing through nature to eternity.

    The lines above are spoken by

    (A) Othello to Desdemona
    (B) Macbeth to Lady Macbeth
    (C) Juliet to Romeo
    (D) King Lear to Cordelia
    (E) Queen Gertrude to Hamlet

102. And he shall judge among the nations, and shall rebuke many people: and they shall beat their swords into plowshares, and their spears into pruninghooks: nation shall not lift up sword against nation, neither shall they learn war any more.

    These words of the King James version of the Bible are from

    (A) Isaiah
    (B) Matthew
    (C) Mark
    (D) Hosea
    (E) Jeremiah

GO ON TO THE NEXT PAGE.

Questions 103-105

I called one day—on Eden's strand
But did not find her—Home—
Surfboarders triumphed in—in Waves—
Archangels of the Foam—

(5) I walked a pace—I tripped across
Browned couples—in cahoots—
No more than Tides need shells to fill
Did they need—bathing suits—

From low boughs—that the Sun kist—hung
(10) A Fruit to taste—at will—
October rustled but—Mankind
Seemed elsewhere gone—to Fall—

103. Which of the following best summarizes the main point that the poem makes about the people of this "Eden's strand" (line 1)?

(A) They are pagan and evil and cannot be redeemed.
(B) They are angelically good and therefore deserve Paradise.
(C) They are amoral and are thus incapable of falling.
(D) They are athletic and strong enough to endure pain.
(E) They are preoccupied with theological questions.

104. The poet mentions October (line 11) in order to

(A) emphasize the ironic contrast between the lateness of the season and the heat of the sun
(B) prepare for a pun on "Fall"—the key word that ends the poem
(C) accurately record when the events of the poem are actually taking place
(D) add a poignant reminder of pleasures past
(E) hint at the illness and decay of the "I" recounting the events

105. The author and title of the poem are, respectively,

(A) X. J. Kennedy and "Emily Dickinson in Southern California"
(B) Allen Ginsberg and "Walt Whitman in a Supermarket in California"
(C) John Berryman and "Homage to Mistress Bradstreet"
(D) Wallace Stevens and "Sunday Morning"
(E) Robert Graves and "To Juan at the Winter Solstice"

106. Cut is the branch that might have grown full straight,
And burnéd is Apollo's laurel bough
That sometime grew within this learnéd man.

These lines follow the death of

(A) Antony
(B) Falstaff
(C) Lucifer
(D) Tamburlaine
(E) Faustus

107. It was Brecht's aim to be entertaining and yet to retain the irony of the source play. His Macheath, the light-fingered, death-dealing leader of a cutthroat gang, is a roguish villain, in some ways the archetypal blackguard of nineteenth-century melodrama. Peachum, the venal chieftain of London's underworld, is Macheath's vengeful father-in-law.

The "source play" mentioned in line 2 is

(A) Gorky's *The Lower Depths*
(B) Aristophanes' *The Wasps*
(C) Gay's *The Beggar's Opera*
(D) Shakespeare's *A Comedy of Errors*
(E) Synge's *The Playboy of the Western World*

GO ON TO THE NEXT PAGE.

Questions 108-111

                Marry, if either the company or indisposition of the
weather bind you to sit the play out, my counsel is then
that you turn plain ape, take up a rush, and tickle the
earnest ears of your fellow gallants, to make other fools
(5) fall a-laughing; mew at passionate speeches, blare at
merry, find fault with the music, whew at the children's
action, whistle at the songs; and above all, curse the fact
that whereas the same day you had bestowed forty
shillings on an embroidered felt and feather (Scotch-
(10) fashion) for your mistress in the court, within two hours
after, you encounter with the very same block on the
stage, when the haberdasher swore to you the impression
was extant but that morning. To conclude, hoard up the
finest play-scraps you can get, upon which your lean wit
(15) may most savourly feed, for want of other stuff, when the
Arcadian and Euphuized gentlewomen have their tongues
sharpened to set upon you.

108. The source of the passage is

(A) a Puritan sermon
(B) a manual for actors
(C) a prologue to a masque
(D) a satirical primer for a would-be gentleman
(E) the stage directions provided for provincial theaters

109. Which of the following is closest in meaning to "Marry" (line 1)?

(A) One should marry
(B) If you are married
(C) Indeed
(D) Regretfully
(E) Meanwhile

110. Lines 7-13 refer to the playgoer's interest in the

(A) latest fashionable mode
(B) morality of theatrical productions
(C) performances of famous actors
(D) latest gossip
(E) mixture of classes in the audience

111. "Arcadian" and "Euphuized" (line 16) refer to works by

(A) Marlowe and Raleigh
(B) Drayton and Ford
(C) Lodge and Bacon
(D) Nashe and Webster
(E) Sidney and Lyly

GO ON TO THE NEXT PAGE.

Questions 112-114

    In pious times, ere priestcraft did begin,
Before polygamy was made a sin;
When man on many multiplied his kind,
....
(5) When nature prompted and no law denied
Promiscuous use of concubine and bride;
Then Israel's monarch after Heaven's own heart,
His vigorous warmth did variously impart
To wives and slaves; and, wide as his command,
Scattered his Maker's image through the land.

112. Which of the following has been omitted at line 4 above?

    (A) Hateful to utter. But what power of mind
    (B) And all the Muses still were in their prime,
    (C) For, God it woot, men may wel often fynde
    (D) As in an organ, from one blast of wind
    (E) Ere one to one was cursedly confined;

113. The "monarch" described in line 7 is

    (A) Noah
    (B) David
    (C) Nebuchadnezzar
    (D) Moses
    (E) Goliath

114. The lines above are the opening of

    (A) Blake's *Jerusalem*
    (B) Byron's "The Vision of Judgment"
    (C) Dryden's *Absalom and Achitophel*
    (D) Milton's *Paradise Regained*
    (E) Tennyson's *Idylls of the King*

115. _____ is the alias of a trickster who poses as a selfless holy man; he induces a pious and pompous bourgeois to part with his money, his house, and his daughter's hand in marriage.

Which of the following is described above?

(A) Raskolnikov
(B) Lafcadio
(C) Mercutio
(D) Tartuffe
(E) Candide

116. Attacks on this genre are nothing new. Back in the 1890's George Bernard Shaw professed himself weary of sitting in the theater and watching "a tailor's advertisement making sentimental remarks to a milliner's advertisement in the middle of an upholsterer and decorator's advertisement." Kenneth Tynan too had much the same complaint. He was, he said, bored with characters who belonged "to a social class derived partly from romantic novels and partly from the playwright's vision of the leisured life he'll lead after his play is a success."

The passage above records attacks on

(A) American melodramas
(B) Drawing-room comedies
(C) The Theater of the Absurd
(D) Brechtian dramas of alienation
(E) Irish political plays

117. The self-concentrated Philanthropist; the high-spirited Woman, bruising herself against the narrow limitations of her sex; the weakly Maiden, whose tremulous nerves endow her with Sibylline attributes; the Minor Poet, beginning life with strenuous aspirations, which die out with his youthful fervor—all these might have been looked for, at Brook Farm, but, by some accident, never made their appearance there.

The passage above is from the preface to

(A) Henry James's *The Portrait of a Lady*
(B) Hawthorne's *The Blithedale Romance*
(C) Twain's *The Mysterious Stranger*
(D) Dreiser's *Sister Carrie*
(E) Crane's *Maggie: A Girl of the Streets*

GO ON TO THE NEXT PAGE.

Questions 118-121

Many were the wit-combats betwixt him
and _____; which two I behold like a Spanish
great galleon and an English man-of-war; _____
(like the former) was built far higher in learning; solid,
(5) but slow, in his performances. _____, with the
English man-of-war, lesser in bulk, but lighter in sailing,
could turn with all tides, tack about, and take advantage
of all winds, by the quickness of his wit and invention.
He died *anno Domini* _____, and was buried at
Stratford-upon-Avon, the town of his nativity.

118. The writer compared to "a Spanish great galleon" is

(A) Jonson
(B) Kyd
(C) Donne
(D) Burton
(E) Pope

119. The writer compared to the "English man-of-war" is

(A) Chaucer
(B) Marlowe
(C) Shakespeare
(D) Bacon
(E) Dryden

120. The comparison of the two men is made by means of

(A) apostrophes
(B) invocations
(C) similes
(D) hyperboles
(E) paradoxes

121. The blank (line 10) immediately after "*anno Domini*" is correctly filled by

(A) 1575
(B) *circa*
(C) 1616
(D) unknown
(E) 1660

Questions 122-123

‹Iesus. M›anne on molde, be meke to me,
And haue thy Maker in þi mynde,
And thynke howe I haue tholid for þe
With pereles paynes for to be pyned.

122. Which of the following is the closest rendering of lines 3 and 4 in the passage?

(A) And remember that I have toiled in order that I might be rewarded with peerless goods and honors.
(B) And I will remember you and think about the pearls and payment that will come to me from you.
(C) And I that am your peerless friend have worked to save you from the burning pyre.
(D) And consider how I have suffered for you, to be tortured with unequaled pains.
(E) And ask if there is anything that will be denied to you, now that you have endured the pangs of love.

123. The passage comes from

(A) *Beowulf*
(B) the Psalms
(C) a Jacobean melodrama
(D) an Elizabethan masque
(E) a medieval mystery play

GO ON TO THE NEXT PAGE.

Questions 124-125

Just as _____, who may have inspired the series, divided the Comédie Humaine into "Scenes of Parisian Life," "Scenes of Provincial Life," and "Scenes of Private Life," so _____ might divide these novels into a number of cycles: one about the planters and their descendants, one about the townspeople of Jefferson, one about the poor whites, one about the Indians, and one about the Negroes.

124. Which of the following will correctly complete line 1 ?

(A) Colette
(B) Sartre
(C) Zola
(D) Camus
(E) Balzac

125. Which of the following will correctly complete line 4 ?

(A) Faulkner
(B) Cather
(C) O'Connor
(D) Twain
(E) Welty

126. Art for Art's Sake! Hail, truest Lord of Hell!
      Hail Genius, Master of the Moral Will!
      The filthiest of paintings painted well
      Is mightier than the purest painted ill
      Yes, mightier than the purest painted well
      So prone are we toward the broad way to Hell.

In relation to "Art for Art's Sake," the lines above reflect

(A) Pound's frankness concerning his debt to the movement
(B) Swinburne's deep admiration for members of the movement who flouted bourgeois morality
(C) Wilde's witty support of the critics who admired and condoned the movement
(D) Tennyson's passionate dislike of the movement
(E) Frost's indignation at the treatment accorded the artists who belonged to the movement

GO ON TO THE NEXT PAGE.

Questions 127-131

FIRST CHARACTER: Detestable *imprimis*! I go to the play in a mask!

SECOND CHARACTER: *Item*, I article, that you continue to like your own face as
(5) long as I shall; and while it passes current with me, that you endeavour not to new-coin it. . . . *Item*, I shut my doors against all bawds with baskets, and pennyworths of muslin, china, fans,
(10) atlases, etc.—*Item*, when you shall be breeding—

FIRST CHARACTER: Ah! name it not.

SECOND CHARACTER: Which may be presumed, with a blessing on our
(15) endeavours—

FIRST CHARACTER: Odious endeavours!

SECOND CHARACTER: I denounce against all strait lacing, squeezing for a shape, till you mold my boy's head like a sugar-loaf. . . .

127. In line 3, the word "article" functions as

(A) a noun
(B) a verb
(C) an adjective
(D) an adverb
(E) a definite article

128. The referent of "Which" in line 13 is

(A) "doors" (line 8)
(B) "atlases" (line 10)
(C) "*Item*" (line 10)
(D) "breeding" (line 11)
(E) "name" (line 12)

129. In lines 15 and 16, "endeavours" means

(A) dieting at meals
(B) professional acting
(C) sexual intercourse
(D) decorous social conduct
(E) a successful lawsuit

130. In the dialogue, the two characters are discussing

(A) ways of reducing their expenses
(B) means of increasing their income
(C) their opportunities for careers in acting
(D) the terms under which they will separate
(E) the conditions under which they will agree to marry

131. The two characters are

(A) Millamant and Mirabell
(B) Margery Pinchwife and Horner
(C) Kate Hardcastle and Marlow
(D) Lady Teazle and Sir Peter Teazle
(E) Beatrice and Benedick

GO ON TO THE NEXT PAGE.

Questions 132-133

My God, my God, thou art a direct God, may I not say a literal God, a God that wouldst be understood literally and according to the plain sense of all that thou sayest? but thou art also (Lord, I intend it to thy glory,
(5) and let no profane misinterpreter abuse it to thy diminution), thou art a figurative, a metaphorical God too; a God in whose words there is such a height of figures, such voyages, such peregrinations to fetch remote and precious metaphors, such extensions, such spreadings,
(10) such curtains of allegories, such third heavens of hyperboles, so harmonious elocutions, so retired and so reserved expressions, so commanding persuasions, so persuading commandments, such sinews even in thy milk, and such things in thy words, as all profane
(15) authors seem of the seed of the serpent that creeps, thou art the Dove that flies.

132. The speaker's principal concern in this passage is to

(A) point out the unreconcilable conflict between God's plain truth and the language used to convey it
(B) indicate that God does not really exist, but is a metaphor
(C) emphasize and delight in the poetic texture of God's Word
(D) defend God's Word against profane authors
(E) pray for help in understanding the complexities of God's Word

133. The passage is by

(A) Blake
(B) Carlyle
(C) Milton
(D) Donne
(E) T. S. Eliot

Questions 134-136 refer to the excerpts below from *The Canterbury Tales*.

134. Which is the moral of the Pardoner's Tale?

135. Which represents the philosophy of the Wife of Bath?

136. Which represents the philosophy of Chauntecleer in the *Nun's Priest's Tale*?

(A) For wedlok is so esy and so clene,
    That in this world it is a paradys.

(B) Wommen desiren to have sovereynetee
    As wel over hir housbond as hir love,
    And for to been in maistrie hym above.

(C) *Radix malorum est cupiditas.*

(D) Thou shalt namoore, thurgh thy flaterye,
    Do me to synge and wynke with myn ye;
    For he that wynketh, whan he sholde see,
    Al wilfully, God lat him nevere thee!

(E) Wommen are born to thraldom and penance,
    And to been under mannes governance.

GO ON TO THE NEXT PAGE.

Questions 137-139

She remembered with what feelings she had prepared for a knowledge of Northanger. She saw that the infatuation had been created, the mischief settled, long before her quitting Bath,
(5) and it seemed as if the whole might be traced to the influence of that sort of reading which she had there indulged.

Charming as were all Mrs. Radcliffe's works, and charming even as were the works of all her
(10) imitators, it was not in them perhaps that human nature, at least in the midland counties of England, was to be looked for. Of the Alps and Pyrenees, with their pine forests and their vices, they might give a faithful delineation; and
(15) Italy, Switzerland, and the South of France, might be as fruitful in horrors as they were there represented. Catherine dared not doubt beyond her own country, and even of that, if hard pressed, would have yielded the northern and
(20) western extremities. But in the central part of England there was surely some security for the existence even of a wife not beloved, in the laws of the land, and the manners of the age. Murder was not tolerated, servants were not slaves, and
(25) neither poison nor sleeping potions to be procured, like rhubarb, from every druggist. Among the Alps and Pyrenees, perhaps, there were no mixed characters. There, such as were not as spotless as an angel, might have the
(30) dispositions of a fiend. But in England it was not so; among the English, she believed, in their hearts and habits, there was a general though unequal mixture of good and bad.

137. The "sort of reading" described in lines 6-17 is best exemplified by

(A) a picaresque novel like *Tom Jones*
(B) a sentimental novel like *The Vicar of Wakefield*
(C) a stream-of-consciousness novel like *Ulysses*
(D) a gothic novel like *The Mysteries of Udolpho*
(E) an epistolary novel like *Pamela*

138. The tone of the author is

(A) aghast and fearful
(B) satiric and ironic
(C) outraged and passionate
(D) xenophobic and vindictive
(E) carping and sorrowful

139. The passage is by

(A) Fielding
(B) Thackeray
(C) Dickens
(D) Smollett
(E) Austen

140. She came out of the rigid agrarian world of Southern Rhodesia which readily makes story-tellers of its exiled children. What British Africa gave her, besides those images of a sky so empty and a society so inflexible as to make the slightest tremor in either worth remarking upon, was a way of perceiving the rest of her life: for a long time to come she could interpret all she saw in terms of "injustice," not merely the injustice of White to Black, of colonizer to colonized, but the more general injustices of class and particularly of sex.

The passage above discusses

(A) Doris Lessing
(B) Flannery O'Connor
(C) Kate Chopin
(D) Sylvia Plath
(E) Elizabeth Bowen

141. Take the "Battle Royal" passage in my novel, where the boys are blindfolded and forced to fight each other for the amusement of the white observers. This is a vital part of behavior patterns in the South, which both Negroes and whites thoughtlessly accept. It is a ritual in preservation of caste lines, a keeping of taboo to appease the gods and ward off bad luck. It is also the initiation ritual to which all greenhorns are subjected. This passage which states what Negroes will see I did not have to invent; the patterns were already there in society, so that all I had to do was present them in a broader context of meaning.

Which of the following accurately describes the passage above?

(A) Morrison is discussing *Song of Solomon*.
(B) Angelou is discussing *I Know Why the Caged Bird Sings*.
(C) Faulkner is discussing *The Sound and the Fury*.
(D) Warren is discussing *All the King's Men*.
(E) Ellison is discussing *Invisible Man*.

GO ON TO THE NEXT PAGE.

Questions 142-144

> Why then, O brawling love! O loving hate!
> O any thing! of nothing first create.
> O heavy lightness! serious vanity!
> Mis-shapen chaos of well-seeming forms!
> (5) Feather of lead, bright smoke, cold fire, sick health!
> Still-waking sleep, that is not what it is!
> This love feel I, that feel no love in this!

142. Which of the following accurately describes the lines?

    (A) Macbeth, despairing of becoming king, resolves to consult the witches.
    (B) Hamlet, angry at Gertrude, vows to kill Rosencrantz.
    (C) Romeo, out of favor with Rosaline, jests about the nature of love.
    (D) Lear, furious with his daughters, attacks Goneril and Regan.
    (E) Othello, in order to please Desdemona, recounts the events of his most recent military engagement.

143. Which of the following is a figure of speech similar to "heavy lightness" (line 3)?

    (A) Promethean labors
    (B) meandering stream
    (C) purple passage
    (D) misspent youth
    (E) thundering silence

144. The passage is characterized by

    (A) a series of oxymorons
    (B) several instances of synaesthesia
    (C) classical references
    (D) color symbolism
    (E) bathos

GO ON TO THE NEXT PAGE.

Questions 145-146

Here is the British public sitting by the writer's side and saying in its vast and unanimous way, "Old women have houses. They have fathers. They have incomes. They have servants. They have hot water bottles. That is
(5) how we know that they are old women. Mr. Wells and Mr. Bennett and Mr. Galsworthy have always taught us that this is the way to recognise them. But now with your Mrs. Brown—how are we to believe her? We do not even know whether her villa was called Albert or
(10) Balmoral; what she paid for her gloves; or whether her mother died of cancer or of consumption. How can she be alive? No; she is a mere figment of your imagination."

And old women of course ought to be made of freehold villas and copyhold estates, not of imagination.

145. The passage is

(A) an attempt to restore the reputations of Wells, Bennett, and Galsworthy
(B) a plea for increased economic opportunities for women
(C) a plea for social justice and increased financial support for the aged and infirm
(D) a protest against the idea that characters are best delineated in terms of the specific external details of their lives
(E) a protest against recent novelists who have aped the style but not the substance of their predecessors

146. The author is

(A) Evelyn Waugh
(B) Flannery O'Connor
(C) Virginia Woolf
(D) Margaret Drabble
(E) Eugene O'Neill

147. _____ represented _____ as the *poète maudit*, the outcast artist in materialistic America whose critical ideas in "The Poetic Principle" and "The Philosophy of Composition" constituted a brilliant aesthetic grounded in an opposition to didactic art.

Which of the following will correctly complete line 1 ?

(A) Goethe . . . Emerson
(B) Mann . . . Melville
(C) Sartre . . . Hawthorne
(D) Barthes . . . Irving
(E) Baudelaire . . . Poe

148. Dorothea and Lydgate are strong characters who painfully learn compassion for their weaker partners. He pays for his mistake of rashly hoping for a compliant angel: "Lydgate had accepted his narrowed lot with sad resignation. He had chosen this fragile creature, and had taken the burthen of her life upon his arms. He must walk as he could, carrying that burthen pitifully." Casaubon, equally, is a fragile creature for whom Dorothea must recognize responsibility. When she struggles with her rage and overcomes it with mercy, she is rewarded by seeing plainly his loneliness and timid affection, and feels "something like the thankfulness that might well up in us if we had narrowly escaped hurting a lamed creature."

The passage above is from a discussion of

(A) Dickens' *Dombey and Son*
(B) Eliot's *Middlemarch*
(C) Thackeray's *Vanity Fair*
(D) Austen's *Sense and Sensibility*
(E) Hardy's *Far from the Madding Crowd*

GO ON TO THE NEXT PAGE.

Questions 149-151 refer to the excerpts below.

149. In which is the speaker Ulysses?

150. In which is the speaker King Lear?

151. In which is the speaker J. Alfred Prufrock?

(A) I am grown peaceful as old age tonight.
I regret little, I would change still less.
Since there my past life lies, why alter it?
The very wrong to Francis!—it is true
I took his coin, was tempted and complied,
And built this house and sinned, and all is said.

(B) . . . you and I are old;
Old age hath yet his honour and his toil;
Death closes all: but something ere the end,
Some work of noble note, may yet be done,
Not unbecoming men that strove with Gods.

(C) Though I have seen my head (grown slightly bald) brought in
      upon a platter,
I am no prophet—and here's no great matter;
I have seen the moment of my greatness flicker,
And I have seen the eternal Footman hold my coat, and snicker,
And in short, I was afraid.

(D) But at my back I always hear
Times's wingèd chariot hurrying near;
And yonder all before us lie
Deserts of vast eternity.

(E) They flattered me like a dog, and told me I had the white hairs in my beard ere the black ones were there. To say "ay" and "no" too was no good divinity. When the rain came to wet me once, and the wind to make me chatter; when the thunder would not peace at my bidding; there I found 'em, there I smelt 'em out. Go to, they are not men o' their words. They told me I was everything. 'Tis a lie—I am not ague-proof.

GO ON TO THE NEXT PAGE.

152. At a crucial point in Ralph Ellison's *Invisible Man*, the protagonist recalls part of a class lecture by one his former professors: "I could hear him: 'Stephen's problem, like ours, was not actually one of creating the uncreated conscience of his race, but of creating the *uncreated features of his face*. Our task is that of making ourselves individuals. The conscience of a race is the gift of its individuals who see, evaluate, record. . . . We create the race by creating ourselves and then to our great astonishment we will have created something far more important: We will have created a culture.'"

In the passage above, the professor is referring to

(A) Dreiser's *An American Tragedy*
(B) James's *The Europeans*
(C) Dickens' *David Copperfield*
(D) Joyce's *A Portrait of the Artist as a Young Man*
(E) Hawthorne's *The Marble Faun*

153. Nay, sure, he's not in hell: he's in Arthur's bosom, if ever man went to Arthur's bosom. A' made a finer end and went away an it had been any christom child; a' parted even just between twelve and one, even at the turning o' the tide; for after I saw him fumble with the sheets and play with flowers and smile upon his fingers' ends, I knew there was but one way; for his nose was as sharp as a pen, and a' babbled of green fields.

The lines above describe the death of

(A) Falstaff
(B) Don Juan
(C) Adonais
(D) Lancelot
(E) Lear

GO ON TO THE NEXT PAGE.

Questions 154-156 refer to the epigraphs below.

154. Which is the epigraph to Wordsworth's *Ode: Intimations of Immortality*?

155. Which is the epigraph to Browning's *Caliban upon Setebos*?

156. Which is the epigraph to T. S. Eliot's *The Hollow Men*?

(A) Late, late yestreen I saw the new Moon,
With the old Moon in her arms;
And I fear, I fear, my Master dear!
We shall have a deadly storm.

(B) Thou hast nor youth nor age
But as it were an after dinner sleep
Dreaming of both.

(C) The Child is father of the Man;
And I could wish my days to be
Bound each to each by natural piety.

(D) 'Thou thoughtest that I was altogether such a one as thyself.'

(E) Mistah Kurtz—he dead.
A penny for the Old Guy.

---

157. Bliss was it in that dawn to be alive,
But to be young was very heaven.

The lines above refer to the

(A) Protestant Reformation
(B) French Revolution
(C) Restoration of Charles II
(D) defeat of the Spanish Armada
(E) Harlem Renaissance

158. Most noble lord, Sir Lancelot of the Lake,
I, sometimes call'd the maid of Astolat,
Come, for you left me taking no farewell,
Hither, to take my last farewell of you.
I loved you, and my love had no return,
And therefore my true love has been my death.

The speaker's name is

(A) Maid Marion
(B) Elaine
(C) Guinevere
(D) Maud
(E) Mariana

GO ON TO THE NEXT PAGE.

Questions 159-161 refer to the passages below.

159. Which describes Shaw's *Pygmalion*?

160. Which describes Beckett's *Waiting for Godot*?

161. Which describes Ibsen's *A Doll's House?*

(A) A small tree stands in the center of an empty stage; there is a hint of a road, and the backdrop is a colorless sky. In the first act, the tree is leafless; in the second it has a few limp leaves. The stage is usually populated by two tramps who spend much of their time discussing whether to remain where they are or go on to some other place.

(B) The stage is bare, even the back wall is visible. Only as the different scenes develop do the actors and the Stage Manager bring on and arrange the chairs, ladders, and boards that are necessary to suggest such places as a soda fountain, the second-floor bedroom windows of the young lovers, and the town cemetery.

(C) The social themes of the play are fully introduced in the first scene when members of the opera audience caught in the rain share a church porch with a cross-section of Londoners that includes sellers, workmen, a retired army officer, and a professor of linguistics.

(D) The setting is modern but strongly reminiscent of classical Greece; the characters wear contemporary dress but with an air of tragic formality. The story of the headstrong girl who defies her tyrannical uncle is taken from Sophocles and retold with strong emphasis on modern parallels.

(E) The somber living room is a reflection of the cautious, conservative husband, officer of a bank in a puritanical, late nineteenth-century city. Christmas decorations bring some life and color into the house, as does the wife's Italian dance costume, but such signs of gaiety are canceled by the death of a dear neighbor and by the husband's discovery that his wife has forged a signature in order to secure a loan.

GO ON TO THE NEXT PAGE.

Questions 162-170. For each of the following passages, identify the author or the work. Base your decision on the content and style of each passage.

162.
　　Here hang I and right and left
　　Two poor fellows hang for theft:
　　All the same's the luck we prove,
　　Though the midmost hangs for love.

(A) Housman's "The Carpenter's Son"
(B) Marvell's "The Definition of Love"
(C) Milton's "On the Morning of Christ's Nativity"
(D) Blake's "The Divine Image"
(E) Hardy's "The Convergence of the Twain"

163. When he [man] is at his very best, he is a sort of low grade nickel-plated angel; at his worst he is unspeakable, unimaginable; and first and last and all the time he is sarcasm. Yet he blandly and in all sincerity calls himself the "noblest work of God" . . . he has talked it through all the ages, and believed it. Believed it, and found nobody among all his race to laugh at it.

(A) Howells
(B) Whitman
(C) Chopin
(D) Hemingway
(E) Twain

164. Art was once the common possession of the whole people; it was the rule in the Middle Ages that the produce of handicraft was beautiful. Doubtless, there were eyesores in the palmy days of medieval art, but these were caused by destruction of wares, not as now by making of them. . . . Ruin bore on its face the tokens of its essential hideousness; to-day it is prosperity that is externally ugly. . . . At present art is only enjoyed, or indeed thought of, by comparatively a few persons, broadly speaking, by the rich and the parasites that minister to them directly. [Art] is helpless and crippled amidst a sea of utilitarian brutality.

(A) Carlyle
(B) Morris
(C) Johnson
(D) Thackeray
(E) Fielding

165.
　　Two things of opposite natures seem to depend
　　On one another, as a man depends
　　On a woman, day on night, the imagined

　　On the real. This is the origin of change.
　　Winter and spring, cold copulars, embrace
　　And forth the particulars of rapture come.

(A) E. E. Cummings
(B) Hart Crane
(C) William Carlos Williams
(D) Wallace Stevens
(E) Robert Frost

166. The story came from an account a certain Mr. Johnson gave me of which I remember this one thing; the remark made by the wife of a farmer he'd gone to see on business; "He's gone to borry some fire." That remark didn't leave me, has never left me. . . . Those words count and signify because they pertain to the lives of those ill-provided times in a poor remote part of Mississippi; they suggested lives of a fallen, larger kind. All the rest—characters, plot, and design of the whole—stemmed all but instantaneously from hearing it spoken.

(A) Eudora Welty
(B) Mary McCarthy
(C) Sarah Orne Jewett
(D) Harriet Beecher Stowe
(E) Willa Cather

167. I've written a play . . . I'll let it lie around and ripen. Writing it was terribly hard work. It has three heroines, you know, each to be a special type, and all three of them are the daughters of a general. The action takes place in a provincial city, on the order of Perm.

(A) Ibsen
(B) Strindberg
(C) Chekhov
(D) Gorky
(E) Pirandello

GO ON TO THE NEXT PAGE.

168. We did not like to declare ourselves women, because—without at that time suspecting that our mode of writing and thinking was not what is called "feminine"—we had a vague impression that authoresses are liable to be looked on with prejudice; we had noticed how critics sometimes use for their chastisement the weapon of personality, and for their reward, a flattery which is not true praise.

    (A) Colette
    (B) Edith Wharton
    (C) Phillis Wheatley
    (D) Jane Austen
    (E) Charlotte Brontë

169. In this posture he was drawn at his just height; and when the picture was fully finished, he caused it to be set by his bed-side, where it continued and became his hourly object till his death and was then given to his dearest friend and executor, Doctor Henry King, then chief residenciary of St. Paul's, who caused him to be thus carved in one entire piece of white marble.

    (A) Boswell's *Life of Johnson*
    (B) Aubrey's *Brief Lives*
    (C) Walton's *Life of Donne*
    (D) Carlyle's *Heroes and Hero-Worship*
    (E) Emerson's *Representative Men*

170. I have no remembrance of the time when I began to learn Greek. I have been told that it was when I was three years old. My earliest recollection on the subject is that of committing to memory what my father termed Vocables, being lists of common Greek words, with their signification in English which he wrote out for me on cards.

    (A) Coleridge
    (B) Mill
    (C) Ruskin
    (D) Wilde
    (E) Arnold

GO ON TO THE NEXT PAGE.

171. Tom and Gatsby, Daisy and Jordan and I, were all
Westerners, and perhaps we possessed some deficiency
in common which made us subtly unadaptable to
Eastern life.

The "I" of the lines above is

(A) Nick Carraway
(B) Ethan Frome
(C) Quentin Compson
(D) Milly Theale
(E) Jake Barnes

Questions 172-173

Banging the coffee-pot into the sink
she hears the angels chiding, and looks out
past the raked gardens to the sloppy sky.
Only a week since They said: *Have no patience.*

(5) The next time it was: *Be insatiable.*
Then: *Save Yourself; others you cannot save.*
Sometimes she's let the tapstream scald her arm,
a match burn to her thumbnail,

or held her hand above the kettle's snout
(10) right in the woolly steam. They are probably angels,
since nothing hurts her anymore, except
each morning's grit blowing into her eyes.

172. Which of the following is syntactically parallel with "let" (line 7)?

(A) "scald" (line 7)
(B) "burn" (line 8)
(C) "held" (line 9)
(D) "are" (line 10)
(E) "hurts" (line 11)

173. Which of the following most accurately describes the woman in the lines above?

(A) She hears voices telling her to resist but does not obey them.
(B) She berates herself for her unkempt appearance and slovenly house, but she lacks the energy to effect an improvement.
(C) She suffers from a loss of religious faith and prays to recover her dedication to lost ideals.
(D) She imagines a full and busy life and the demands that a husband and children would make of her.
(E) She is so overtaxed that she is subject to frequent accidents in the kitchen.

GO ON TO THE NEXT PAGE.

Questions 174-175

Two statements in his address at the Cotton States Exposition at Atlanta in 1895 gained wide currency among Black and White Americans, and became central to the contemporary controversy, whether in literature
(5) or matters of political and social policy, about the future of Blacks in America. _____ declared: "Cast down your bucket where you are," and "In all things that are purely social we [Blacks and Whites] can be as separate as the fingers, yet one as the hand in all things essential to mutual progress."

174. The name that correctly fills the blank in line 6 is

(A) Frederick Douglass
(B) W.E.B. Du Bois
(C) Marcus Garvey
(D) Booker T. Washington
(E) Paul Laurence Dunbar

175. An opponent who eloquently attacked this spokesman and his point of view in *The Souls of Black Folk* is

(A) Marcus Garvey
(B) James Weldon Johnson
(C) George Washington Carver
(D) Countee Cullen
(E) W.E.B. Du Bois

Questions 176-178

Below are three excerpts from Shakespeare's plays, each of which owes its existence in part to one of the characteristics of dramatic productions at the Globe Theatre. Match each excerpt with the characteristic it reflects.

THE CHARACTERISTICS

(A) There were no actresses in the theater companies.
(B) There were no furnished interiors for sets.
(C) Poetic description took the place of lighting effects.
(D) Plots of tragedies were regarded as true; of comedies, as fictitious.
(E) A known liar spoke the truth when delivering a soliloquy.

176. But look, the morn in russet mantle clad
Walks o'er the dew of yon high eastward hill.

177.   I shall see
Some squeaking Cleopatra boy my greatness
I'th' posture of a whore.

178. Thus do I ever make my fool my purse;
For I mine own gain'd knowledge should profane
If I would time expend with such a snipe
But for my sport and profit. I hate the Moor.

GO ON TO THE NEXT PAGE.

Questions 179-181 refer to the excerpts below.

179. Which refers to Leda?

180. Which refers to Daphne?

181. Which refers to Europa?

(A) . . . . . and on his backe
 Her through the sea did beare; so lively scene
 That it true Sea, and true Bull ye would weene.

(B) . . . her limbs grew numb and heavy, her soft breasts
 Were closed with delicate bark, her hair was leaves,
 Her arms were branches, and her speedy feet
 Rooted and held, and her head became a tree top,
 Everything gone except her grace, her shining.

(C) A sudden blow: the great wings beating still
 Above the staggering girl, her thighs caressed
 By the dark webs, her nape caught in his bill,
 He holds her helpless breast upon his breast.

(D) . . . the god hid the land in a dark cloud,
 Caught the fleeing girl and took her by force.

(E) Queen and Huntress, chaste and fair,
  Now the sun is laid to sleep,
 Seated in thy silver chair,
  State in wonted manner keep:
   Hesperus entreats thy light,
   Goddess excellently bright.

GO ON TO THE NEXT PAGE.

182. For Gwendolen and Cecily this important name has "an irresistible fascination" which inspires "absolute confidence." It is a "divine" name with "a music of its own," the "only really safe name." So eager are Jack and Algernon to win the hearts of Gwendolen and Cecily that they would risk the grave dangers of being christened in order that they might possess that name—and its admirers.

The name is

(A) Dorimant
(B) Tristan
(C) Dorian
(D) Ernest
(E) Ishmael

Questions 183-185

As for Us, . . . We are content with the Bee, to pretend to Nothing of our own, beyond our Wings and our Voice: that is to say, our Flights and our Language; For the rest, whatever we have got, has been by infinite
(5) Labor, and search, and ranging thro' every Corner of Nature: The Difference is, that instead of Dirt and Poison, we have rather chose to fill our Hives with Honey and Wax, thus furnishing Mankind with the Noblest of Things, which are Sweetness and Light.

183. The passage refers to the

(A) relationship between mythology and religion
(B) dispute between the Ancients and the Moderns
(C) necessity for candor in autobiography
(D) healing powers of elegiac and pastoral poetry
(E) theory of humors

184. "Sweetness and Light" (line 9) stand for

(A) respect and honesty
(B) delight and instruction
(C) labor and rewards
(D) sentimentality and sentiment
(E) pride and humility

185. The passage appears in

(A) Ruskin's *Stones of Venice*
(B) Wordsworth's Preface to the *Lyrical Ballads*
(C) Carlyle's *Past and Present*
(D) Arnold's *Culture and Anarchy*
(E) Swift's *The Battle of the Books*

GO ON TO THE NEXT PAGE.

Questions 186-188. Match the thematic passages below with the title of the novel in which each appears.

(The titles appear after 188.)

186. Masked parties, Savage parties, Victorian parties, Greek parties, parties where one had to dress as somebody else, almost naked parties in St. John's Wood, parties in flats and studios and houses and ships and hotels and night clubs, in windmills and swimming baths . . . all that succession and repetition of massed humanity.

187. "He never took the sacraments, he never married his wife in church. I think he died in what we are told is mortal sin—I'm not sure." He sighed and whistled, bending his old head. He said, "You can't conceive, my child, nor can I or anyone—the appalling . . . strangeness of the mercy of God."

188. Sharp, clear electric lights at Stacks Gate! An undefinable quick of evil in them! And all the unease, the ever-shifting dread of the industrial night in the Midlands.

(A) Orwell's *1984*
(B) Lawrence's *Lady Chatterley's Lover*
(C) Forster's *Howards End*
(D) Waugh's *Vile Bodies*
(E) Greene's *Brighton Rock*

Questions 189-192

"So, reverend Sir, you have made a visit into the forest," observed the witch-lady, nodding her high head-dress at him. "The next time, I pray you to allow me only a fair warning, and I
(5) shall be proud to bear you company. Without taking overmuch upon myself, my good word will go far towards gaining any strange gentleman a fair reception from yonder potentate you wot of!"
(10) "I profess, madam," answered the clergyman, with a grave obeisance, such as the lady's rank demanded, and his own good-breeding made imperative,—"I profess, on my conscience and character, that I am utterly bewildered as
(15) touching the purport of your words! I went not into the forest to seek a potentate; neither do I, at any future time, design a visit thither, with a view to gaining the favour of such personage. My one sufficient object was to greet that pious
(20) friend of mine, the Apostle Eliot, and rejoice with him over the many precious souls he hath won from heathendom!"

189. The "potentate" (line 8) is

(A) the Apostle Eliot
(B) the Devil
(C) the Archangel Michael
(D) the Angelic host
(E) Jesus

190. A modern equivalent of *wot* (line 9) is

(A) hear
(B) speak
(C) know
(D) are afraid
(E) are fond

GO ON TO THE NEXT PAGE.

191. In his defense the clergyman claims that he has entered the forest in order to

   (A) celebrate the success of a missionary enterprise
   (B) avoid political involvement in the secular affairs of his parish
   (C) examine the state of his conscience in natural surroundings
   (D) pray for the redemption of his sinful parishioners
   (E) prepare a sermon that will unify his divided parish

192. This exchange takes place between

   (A) Thomas Gradgrind and Sissie Jupe
   (B) Rochester and Jane Eyre
   (C) Silas Marner and Eppie
   (D) Arthur Dimmesdale and Mistress Hibben
   (E) Clym Yeobright and Eustacia Vye

193. "Full of the illusions of ignorance and youth," the novel's heroine enters the great city, her heart "troubled by a kind of terror." Instead of a "world of light and merriment," she finds "the grimness of shift and toil." There is no moral order here, only the order of nature, the marketplace, solitary strivings and defeats. Chicago's boulevards and plate-glass windows, glittering restaurants, hotels, theaters, and department stores are only the farther reaches of the shanties and coal yards she passes on her walks, the factories and sweatshops where she looks for work, "the drag of a lean and narrow life" she feels in the flat she shares.

   The passage above is from a discussion of

   (A) James's *The Portrait of a Lady*
   (B) Hemingway's *For Whom the Bell Tolls*
   (C) Bellow's *Henderson the Rain King*
   (D) Dreiser's *Sister Carrie*
   (E) Hawthorne's *The Blithedale Romance*

194. He dwelt particularly on the *Essay on Vision* as a masterpiece of analytical reasoning. So it undoubtedly is. He was exceedingly angry with Dr. Johnson for striking the stone with his foot, in allusion to this author's theory of Matter and Spirit, and saying, "Thus I confute him, Sir."

   Which of the following accurately describes the passage above?

   (A) Arnold is discussing Dryden's opinion of Donne.
   (B) Wordsworth is discussing Pope's opinion of Swift.
   (C) Eliot is discussing Pound's opinion of Aristotle.
   (D) Lamb is discussing Blake's opinion of Milton.
   (E) Hazlitt is discussing Coleridge's opinion of Bishop Berkeley.

195. The gift is loved but not the gifted one.
   The coat of many colors is much admired
   By everyone, but he who wears the coat
   Is not made warm.

   The passage above refers to the story of

   (A) Joseph and His Brothers
   (B) Abraham and Isaac
   (C) Judith and Holofernes
   (D) the Prodigal Son
   (E) Jacob and Esau

GO ON TO THE NEXT PAGE.

Questions 196-200

Not mine own fears, nor the prophetic soul
Of the wide world, dreaming on things to come,
Can yet the lease of my true love control,
Suppos'd as forfeit to a confin'd doom.
(5) The mortal moon hath her eclipse endur'd
And the sad augurs mock their own presage,
Incertainties now crown themselves assur'd,
And peace proclaims olives of endless age.
Now with the drops of this most balmy time
(10) My love looks fresh, and Death to me subscribes,
Since spite of him I'll live in this poor rhyme,
While he insults o'er dull and speechless tribes;
And thou in this shalt find thy monument,
When tyrants' crests and tombs of brass are spent.

196. Which of the following is the best paraphrase of line 4?

(A) Once thought of as subject to a fate that would limit its duration
(B) Eternally doomed to perpetual and ignominious failure
(C) Now seen to be predestined to a life imprisoned in poverty
(D) Unfortunately placed in jeopardy by an unkind fate that has proved to be implacable
(E) Discarded by a fickle and cruel lover who has become irresistible

197. Which of the following is the best paraphrase of line 7?

(A) Desirable events that were once doubtful are so no longer.
(B) Uncertainties, long ignored and dreaded, are now confirmed.
(C) The status quo is confirmed and certain to continue indefinitely.
(D) Those of little merit are exalted and admired without reservation.
(E) The monarchy endures with renewed glory and power.

198. The closest paraphrase of "to me subscribes" (line 10) is

(A) opposes me
(B) surrenders to me
(C) cooperates with me
(D) evades me
(E) enlists under me

199. The closest synonym for "insults" (line 12) is

(A) denigrates
(B) argues
(C) triumphs
(D) languishes
(E) broods

200. Which of the following most nearly duplicates the idea the last two lines?

(A) And nothing 'gainst Time's scythe can make defen[ce]
Save breed, to brave him when he takes thee hence
(B) So long as men can breathe or eyes can see,
So long lives this and this gives life to thee.
(C) O learn to read what silent love hath writ:
To hear with eyes belongs to love's fine wit.
(D) For thy sweet love remembered such wealth brings
That then I scorn to change my state with kings.
(E) If thy unworthiness rais'd love in me,
More worthy I to be belov'd of thee.

GO ON TO THE NEXT PAGE.

Questions 201-202

It is not to be considered as the effusions of real passion; for passion runs not after remote allusions and obscure opinions. Passion plucks no berries from the myrtle and ivy, nor calls upon Arethuse and Mincius, nor tells of "rough satyrs and fauns with cloven heel." Where there is leisure for fiction there is little grief.

201. In the passage, Johnson is discussing

   (A) Chaucer's "Complaint to his Purse"
   (B) Marlowe's *Dr. Faustus*
   (C) Shakespeare's *Love's Labour's Lost*
   (D) Donne's "A Valediction: Forbidding Mourning"
   (E) Milton's "Lycidas"

202. Johnson is criticizing the work for its

   (A) inaccurate allusions
   (B) unrestrained emotionalism
   (C) lack of fictional elements
   (D) mechanical use of pastoral convention
   (E) lack of a realistic natural setting

203. The general form of his prose work is found in his so-called *ficciones*, which are really precisely wrought essays on imaginary and nonexistent subjects. The form he chose to imitate was usually that of the scholarly article. His great fascination with mathematical and semantic models of the universe is expressed in his labyrinths and the arcana of numerology and cabalistic mysticism.

The author discussed above is

   (A) Carlos Fuentes
   (B) Jorge Luis Borges
   (C) Gabriel García Márquez
   (D) Mario Vargas Llosa
   (E) Federico García Lorca

Questions 204-205

Despite the apocalyptic tone and impassioned advocacy of such collections as *Notes of a Native Son* (1955) and *The Fire Next Time* (1963), he insisted that he was "a witness to the truth" rather than a spokesman for a people. "I depended on neither the white world nor the black world," he said in describing his struggle for psychological survival and his expatriation to Paris: "I had to say, 'A plague on both your houses!'"

204. In calling down "A plague on both your houses," the writer compares himself to

   (A) Edmund in *King Lear*
   (B) Ophelia in *Hamlet*
   (C) Hotspur in *Henry IV*, *Part 1*
   (D) Anne in *Richard III*
   (E) Mercutio in *Romeo and Juliet*

205. The writer discussed in the passage is

   (A) James Baldwin
   (B) Countee Cullen
   (C) Ralph Ellison
   (D) Langston Hughes
   (E) Norman Mailer

GO ON TO THE NEXT PAGE.

206. *It befel in the dayes of Vther pendragon when he was kynge of all Englond / and fo regned that there was a myzty duke of Cornewaill that helde warre ageynft hym long tyme / And the duke was called the duke of Tyntagil / and fo by meanes kynge Vther fend for this duk / chargyng hym to brynge his wyf with hym / for fhe was called a fair lady / and a paffynge wyfe / and her name was called Igrayne /*

The passage above begins

(A) *Beowulf*
(B) *Sir Gawain and the Green Knight*
(C) Spenser's *Faerie Queene*
(D) Chaucer's *Troilus and Criseyde*
(E) Malory's *Morte D'Arthur*

207. In *Lolita*, Humbert Humbert describes himself as "resting his head on his hand and burning with desire and dyspepsia." The figure of language that Humbert employs is also used in which of the following?

(A) The spendthrift crocus, bursting through the mould,
    Naked and shivering, with his cup of gold
(B) Go and catch a falling star,
    Get with child a mandrake root,
(C) Here thou, great Anna! whom three realms obey,
    Dost sometimes counsel take—and sometimes tea.
(D) The years to come seemed waste of breath,
    A waste of breath the years behind.
(E) If with such talents Heaven hath blessed 'em,
    Have I not reason to detest 'em?

GO ON TO THE NEXT PAGE.

Questions 208-209

> John Synge, I, and Augusta Gregory thought
> All that we did, all that we said or sang
> Must come from contact with the soil, from that
> Contact everything Antaeus-like grew strong.
> We three alone in modern times had brought
> Everything down to that sole test again,
> Dream of the noble and the beggarman.

208. The "I" of the lines above is

(A) Pound
(B) Yeats
(C) Hopkins
(D) T. S. Eliot
(E) D. H. Lawrence

209. Which of the following also describes Antaeus (line 4) ?

(A) . . . scal'd the sky
   And forc'd great Jove from his own heaven to fly,
   (What king, what crown from treason's reach is free,
   If Jove and heaven can violated be?)

(B) Sky-born and royal
   snake-choker, dung-heaver,
   his mind big with golden apples,
   his future hung with trophies.

(C) Ageless, lusty, he twists into bull, ram, serpent,
   Swan, gold rain; a hundred wily disguises
   To catch girl, nymph, or goddess.

(D) He stood in the zephyr, pipes in hand,
   On a height of naked pasture land;
   In all the country he did command
   He saw no smoke and he saw no roof.
   That was well! and he stamped a hoof.

(E) . . . oft foiled still rose,
   Receiving from his mother Earth new strength,
   Fresh from his fall, and fiercer grapple joined,
   Throttled at length in the air, expired and fell.

GO ON TO THE NEXT PAGE.

210. She is a small-time businesswoman who runs a wagon canteen. She survives a holocaust by exploiting both war and peace, victors and vanquished, for modest financial sustenance. She is neither villainess nor heroine but "a great living contradiction." Though she will do anything to assure her children's survival, she nonetheless loses her two sons when she haggles too long over business deals.

    The passage above describes

    (A) Brecht's Mother Courage
    (B) Ibsen's Hedda Gabler
    (C) Gay's Mrs. Peachum
    (D) Sheridan's Lydia Languish
    (E) Shaw's Major Barbara

211. I became a playwright when I tried the impossible—to learn to speak English. My textbook informed me that the floor was under my feet and the ceiling above my head, which gave me vertigo. In the same book I became acquainted with two typical British families, the interchangeable Smiths and Martins. Taking over from me, they dictated a play that I took to be the tragedy of language. When I heard the first-night audience laugh, I realized it was a comedy.

    Which of the following correctly describes the passage above?

    (A) Lorca is discussing *The House of Bernarda Alba*.
    (B) Genet is discussing *The Blacks*.
    (C) Strindberg is discussing *The Father*.
    (D) Ionesco is discussing *The Bald Soprano*.
    (E) Pirandello is discussing *Six Characters in Search of an Author*.

212. "If one designs to construct a dwelling house," he wrote, "it behooves him to exercise a little Yankee shrewdness, lest after all he finds himself in a workhouse, a labyrinth without a clue, a museum, an almshouse, a prison or a splendid mausoleum instead." With borrowed tools and borrowed land he built himself a 10- by 15-foot cabin—a palace considering his belief that even a 3- by 6-foot toolbox would by no means be a "despicable alternative" house.

    The passage above describes

    (A) Emerson
    (B) Melville
    (C) Thoreau
    (D) Hawthorne
    (E) Poe

GO ON TO THE NEXT PAGE.

213. Hopkins' *sprung rhythm* is the substitution of
    (A) sibilant rhyme for hovering rhyme
    (B) a system of stress for a system of poetic feet
    (C) a system of linking rhymes for a system of speech rhythms
    (D) the language of everyday discourse for the language of poetry
    (E) phrases and clauses for what is normally expressed by inflections

214. Rebellion in her case does not have the epic dimension of that of the masculine heroes of the nineteenth-century novel, yet it is no less heroic. Hers is the rebellion of an individual, and to all appearances a self-centered one: she violates the codes of her milieu because she is driven to do so by problems that are hers alone, not in the name of all humanity, of a certain ethic or ideology. It is because she feels that society is fettering her imagination, her body, her dreams, her appetites that she suffers, commits adultery, lies, steals, and in the end kills herself.

    In the passage above, Mario Vargas Llosa describes
    (A) Moll Flanders
    (B) Sister Carrie
    (C) Mrs. Dalloway
    (D) Emma Bovary
    (E) Milly Theale

Questions 215-216

1915: February

The smeared, leather-coated, leather-greaved engineer
Walks in front of his traction-engine
Like some figure out of the sagas,
Like Grettir or like Skarpheddin,
(5) With a sort of majestical swagger.
And his machine lumbers after him
Like some mythological beast,
Like Grendel bewitched and in chains,
But his ill luck will make me no sagas,
(10) Nor will you crack the riddle of his skull,
O you over-educated, over-refined literati!

Copyright 1988. Reprinted by permission of the Ezra Pound Literary Trust.

215. In line 1, "greaved" refers to the engineer's
    (A) headgear
    (B) grieving face
    (C) gravity of demeanor
    (D) grace under pressure
    (E) leg protectors

216. In line 8, "Grendel" refers to
    (A) King Arthur's sword
    (B) a monster Beowulf kills
    (C) Duessa's henchman
    (D) the enemy of Sir Gawain
    (E) Robin Hood's persecutor

GO ON TO THE NEXT PAGE.

Questions 217-220

```
                              As an eagle grasped
                 In folds of the green serpent, feels her breast
                 Burn with the poison, and precipitates
                 Through night and day, tempest, and calm, and cloud,
           (5)   Frantic with dizzying anguish, her blind flight
                 O'er the wide aëry wilderness:  thus driven
                 By the bright shadow of that lovely dream,
                 Beneath the cold glare of the desolate night,
                 Through tangled swamps and deep precipitous dells,
          (10)   Startling with careless step the moon-light snake,
                 He fled.
```

217. The object of "precipitates" (line 3) is

   (A) "tempest" (line 4)
   (B) "cloud" (line 4)
   (C) "anguish" (line 5)
   (D) "flight" (line 5)
   (E) "wilderness" (line 6)

218. In line 6, "driven" modifies

   (A) "eagle" (line 1)
   (B) "serpent" (line 2)
   (C) "flight" (line 5)
   (D) "wilderness" (line 6)
   (E) "He" (line 11)

219. The passage is best described as an example of

   (A) antithesis
   (B) irony
   (C) a parable
   (D) an extended simile
   (E) the pathetic fallacy

220. The author of the passage is

   (A) Milton
   (B) Shelley
   (C) Tennyson
   (D) Spenser
   (E) Housman

GO ON TO THE NEXT PAGE.

Questions 221-225

    For this, ere Phoebus rose, he had implored
Propitious Heaven, and every power adored,
But chiefly Love—to Love an altar built,
Of twelve vast French romances, neatly gilt.
(5) There lay three garters, half a pair of gloves,
And all the trophies of his former loves.
With tender billet-doux he lights the pyre,
And breathes three amorous sighs to raise the fire.
Then prostrate falls, and begs with ardent eyes
(10) Soon to obtain, and long possess the prize:
The powers gave ear, and granted half his prayer,
The rest the winds dispersed in empty air.

221. Lines 4-7 describe objects that

    (A) are used in a sacrificial rite designed to ensure success
    (B) are associated with the pagan cult of Phoebus
    (C) he destroys as painful reminders of failed love affairs
    (D) represent the scholarly life that he now despises
    (E) prove to him that his wife has been unfaithful

222. The subject of "built" (line 3) is

    (A) "this" (line 1)
    (B) "he" (line 1)
    (C) "Heaven" (line 2)
    (D) "power" (line 2)
    (E) "altar" (line 3)

223. Lines 11-12 suggest that

    (A) the powers are totally indifferent to his suffering
    (B) divine forgiveness alone can absolve him of his sins
    (C) he has delayed too long in seeking assistance from Heaven
    (D) he will gain but not be able to keep the thing he seeks
    (E) the powers will first test him to see whether he is worthy of their aid

224. The "prize" (line 10) is a

    (A) handkerchief
    (B) green garter
    (C) lady's fan
    (D) fur muff
    (E) lock of hair

225. The passage is written in

    (A) terza rima
    (B) ottava rima
    (C) heroic couplets
    (D) blank verse
    (E) alliterative verse

GO ON TO THE NEXT PAGE.

Questions 226-227

Thackeray is a big fellow, soul and body; of many gifts and qualities (particularly in the Hogarth line, with a dash of Sterne superadded), of enormous *appetite* withal, and very uncertain and chaotic in all points except his *outer breeding*, which is fixed enough, and perfect according to the modern English style. . . . A *big*, fierce, weeping, hungry man.

226. The mention of Hogarth (line 2) in this character sketch implies that Thackeray's work is marked by

(A) social satire
(B) picturesque settings
(C) mawkish sentimentality
(D) meretricious heroism
(E) lachrymose hypocrisy

227. The mention of Sterne (line 3) implies that Thackeray's work combines

(A) melancholy and morbidity
(B) morality and didacticism
(C) psychological analysis and tragedy
(D) simplicity and conventionality
(E) humor and sentiment

GO ON TO THE NEXT PAGE.

Questions 228-230 refer to the following passages.

228. Which is by Arnold?

229. Which is by T.S. Eliot?

230. Which is by Shelley?

(A) The strongest part of our religion today is its unconscious poetry.... We should conceive of poetry worthily, and more highly than it has been the custom to conceive of it. We should conceive of it as capable of higher uses, and called to higher destinies, than those which in general men have assigned to it hitherto. More and more mankind will discover that we have to turn to poetry to interpret life for us, to console us, to sustain us.

(B) Poetry is not a turning loose of emotion, but an escape from emotion; it is not the expression of personality, but an escape from personality. But, of course, only those who have personality and emotions know what it means to want to escape from these things.

(C) [Poets are] the happiest, the best, the wisest, and the most illustrious of men . . . men of the most spotless virtue, of the most consummate prudence . . . the hierophants of an unapprehended inspiration; the mirrors of the gigantic shadows which futurity casts upon the present; the words which express what they understand not; the trumpets which sing to battle and feel not what they inspire; the influence which is moved not, but moves. Poets are the unacknowledged legislators of the world.

(D) [The Poet is] a man speaking to men: a man, it is true, endued with more lively sensibility, more enthusiasm and tenderness, who has a greater knowledge of human nature, and a more comprehensive soul, than are supposed to be common among mankind. . . . In spite of difference of soil and climate, of language and manners, of laws and customs, in spite of things silently gone out of mind and things violently destroyed, the Poet binds together by passion and knowledge the vast empire of human society.

(E) The poet makes himself a *seer* by a long, prodigious, and rational *disordering* of *all the senses*. Every form of love, of suffering, of madness; he searches himself, he consumes all the poisons in him, and keeps only their quintessences. This is an unspeakable torture during which he needs all his faith and superhuman strength, and during which he becomes the great patient, the great criminal, the great accursed—and the great learned one!—among men.—For he arrives at the *unknown*! Because he has cultivated his own soul—which was rich to begin with—more than any other man!

IF YOU FINISH BEFORE TIME IS CALLED, YOU MAY CHECK YOUR WORK ON THIS TEST.

NO TEST MATERIAL ON THIS PAGE

NOTE: To ensure prompt processing of test results, it is important that you fill in the blanks <u>exactly</u> as directed.

SUBJECT TEST

A. Print and sign your full name in this box:

PRINT: _____
(LAST)   (FIRST)   (MIDDLE)

SIGN: _____

Copy this code in box 6 on your answer sheet. Then fill in the corresponding ovals exactly as shown.

Copy the Test Name and Form Code in box 7 on your answer sheet.

TEST NAME *Literature in English*

FORM CODE *GR9064*

GRADUATE RECORD EXAMINATIONS SUBJECT TEST

B. The Subject Tests are intended to measure your achievement in a specialized field of study. Most of the questions are concerned with subject matter that is probably familiar to you, but some of the questions may refer to areas that you have not studied.

Your score will be determined by subtracting one-fourth the number of incorrect answers from the number of correct answers. Questions for which you mark no answer or more than one answer are not counted in scoring. If you have some knowledge of a question and are able to rule out one or more of the answer choices as incorrect, your chances of selecting the correct answer are improved, and answering such questions will likely improve your score. It is unlikely that pure guessing will raise you score; it may lower your score.

You are advised to use your time effectively and to work as rapidly as you can without losing accuracy. Do not spend too much time on questions that are too difficult for you. Go on to the other questions and come back to the difficult ones later if you can.

YOU MUST INDICATE ALL YOUR ANSWERS ON THE SEPARATE ANSWER SHEET. No credit will be given for anything written in this examination book, but you may write in the book as much as you wish to work out your answers. After you have decided on your response to a question, fill in the corresponding oval on the answer sheet. BE SURE THAT EACH MARK IS DARK AND COMPLETELY FILLS THE OVAL. Mark <u>only one</u> answer to each question. No credit will be given for multiple answers. Erase all stray marks. If you change an answer, be sure that all previous marks are erased completely. Incomplete erasures may be read as intended answers. Do not be concerned that the answer sheet provides spaces for more answers than there are questions in the test.

Example:

What city is the capital of France?

(A) Rome
(B) Paris
(C) London
(D) Cairo
(E) Oslo

Sample Answer

CORRECT ANSWER PROPERLY MARKED

IMPROPER MARKS

DO NOT OPEN YOUR TEST BOOK UNTIL YOU ARE TOLD TO DO SO.

GRADUATE RECORD EXAMINATIONS® - GRE® - SUBJECT TEST

SIDE 1

DO NOT USE INK

Use only a pencil with soft, black lead (No. 2 or HB) to complete this answer sheet.
Be sure to fill in completely the space that corresponds to your answer choice.
Completely erase any errors or stray marks.

1. NAME

Enter your last name, first name initial (given name), and middle initial if you have one.
Omit spaces, apostrophes, Jr., II, etc.

Last Name (Family or Surname) - first 15 letters | F.I. | M.I.

2. YOUR NAME:
(Print) Last Name (Family or Surname) First Name (Given) M.I.

MAILING ADDRESS:
(Print)
P.O. Box or Street Address
City   State or Province
Country   Zip or Postal Code

CENTER:
City   State or Province
Country   Center Number   Room Number

3. DATE OF BIRTH
Month / Day / Year
Jan., Feb., Mar., April, May, June, July, Aug., Sept., Oct., Nov., Dec.

4. SOCIAL SECURITY NUMBER
(U.S.A. only)

5. REGISTRATION NUMBER
(from your admission ticket)

6. TITLE CODE
(from middle of back cover of your test book)

7. TEST NAME (on back cover of your test book)

8. TEST BOOK SERIAL NUMBER
(red number in upper right corner of front cover of your test book)

FORM CODE (on back cover of your test book)

SHADED AREA FOR ETS USE ONLY

BE SURE EACH MARK IS DARK AND COMPLETELY FILLS THE INTENDED SPACE AS ILLUSTRATED HERE: ●
YOU MAY FIND MORE RESPONSE SPACES THAN YOU NEED. IF SO, PLEASE LEAVE THEM BLANK.

1–38 (A)(B)(C)(D)(E)   39–76 (A)(B)(C)(D)(E)   77–114 (A)(B)(C)(D)(E)

Item responses continued on reverse side.

Copyright © 1992 by Educational Testing Service, Princeton, NJ 08541.

54074 • 02954 • TF72P150e

MH92209

I.N. 275448

Q2546-06

SIDE 2

SUBJECT TEST

COMPLETE THE CERTIFICATION STATEMENT, THEN TURN ANSWER SHEET OVER TO SIDE 1.

CERTIFICATION STATEMENT
Please write the following statement below, DO NOT PRINT.
"I certify that I am the person whose name appears on this answer sheet. I also agree not to disclose the contents of the test I am taking today to anyone."
Sign and date where indicated.

SIGNATURE: _____ DATE: __/__/__
                                              Month Day Year

BE SURE EACH MARK IS DARK AND COMPLETELY FILLS THE INTENDED SPACE AS ILLUSTRATED HERE: ●
YOU MAY FIND MORE RESPONSE SPACES THAN YOU NEED. IF SO, PLEASE LEAVE THEM BLANK.

Questions 115–242, each with options (A) (B) (C) (D) (E).

IF YOU DO NOT WANT THIS ANSWER SHEET TO BE SCORED

If you want to cancel your scores from this administration, complete A and B below. No record of this test will be sent to the recipients you indicated, and there will be no scores on your GRE file. You will receive confirmation of this cancellation; you will **not** receive scores for this test. Once a score is canceled, it cannot be reinstated.

To cancel your scores from this test administration, you must:
A. fill in both ovals here ..... ○ – ○   B. sign your full name here: _____

TR	TW	TFS	TCS	1R	1W	1FS	1CS	2R	2W	2FS	2CS
FOR ETS USE ONLY				3R	3W	3FS	3CS	4R	4W	4FS	4CS
				5R	5W	5FS	5CS	6R	6W	6FS	6CS

GRADUATE RECORD EXAMINATIONS® - GRE® - SUBJECT TEST

SIDE 1

DO NOT USE INK

Use only a pencil with soft, black lead (No. 2 or HB) to complete this answer sheet.
Be sure to fill in completely the space that corresponds to your answer choice.
Completely erase any errors or stray marks.

1. NAME
Enter your last name, first name initial (given name), and middle initial if you have one.
Omit spaces, apostrophes, Jr., II., etc.

Last Name (Family or Surname) - first 15 letters | FI | MI

2. YOUR NAME: (Print)
Last Name (Family or Surname) | First Name (Given) | M.I.

MAILING ADDRESS: (Print)
P.O. Box or Street Address
City | State or Province
Country | Zip or Postal Code

CENTER:
City | State or Province
Country | Center Number | Room Number

3. DATE OF BIRTH
Month: Jan., Feb., Mar., April, May, June, July, Aug., Sept., Oct., Nov., Dec.
Day | Year

4. SOCIAL SECURITY NUMBER (U.S.A. only)

5. REGISTRATION NUMBER (from your admission ticket)

6. TITLE CODE (from middle of back cover of your test book)

7. TEST NAME (on back cover of your test book)

FORM CODE (on back cover of your test book)

8. TEST BOOK SERIAL NUMBER (red number in upper right corner of front cover of your test book)

SHADED AREA FOR ETS USE ONLY

BE SURE EACH MARK IS DARK AND COMPLETELY FILLS THE INTENDED SPACE AS ILLUSTRATED HERE: ●
YOU MAY FIND MORE RESPONSE SPACES THAN YOU NEED. IF SO, PLEASE LEAVE THEM BLANK.

1–38, 39–76, 77–114: (A) (B) (C) (D) (E)

Item responses continued on reverse side.

Copyright © 1992 by Educational Testing Service, Princeton, NJ 08541.

54074 • 02954 • TF72P150e
MH92209
I.N. 275448
Q2546-06

SIDE 2

SUBJECT TEST

COMPLETE THE CERTIFICATION STATEMENT, THEN TURN ANSWER SHEET OVER TO SIDE 1.

CERTIFICATION STATEMENT
Please write the following statement below, DO NOT PRINT.
"I certify that I am the person whose name appears on this answer sheet. I also agree not to disclose the contents of the test I am taking today to anyone."
Sign and date where indicated.

SIGNATURE: _____   DATE: ___/___/___
                                                Month Day Year

BE SURE EACH MARK IS DARK AND COMPLETELY FILLS THE INTENDED SPACE AS ILLUSTRATED HERE: ●.
YOU MAY FIND MORE RESPONSE SPACES THAN YOU NEED. IF SO, PLEASE LEAVE THEM BLANK.

[Answer bubbles numbered 115–242, each with options A B C D E]

IF YOU DO NOT WANT THIS ANSWER SHEET TO BE SCORED

If you want to cancel your scores from this administration, complete A and B below. No record of this test will be sent to the recipients you indicated, and there will be no scores on your GRE file. You will receive confirmation of this cancellation; you will **not** receive scores for this test. Once a score is canceled, it cannot be reinstated.

To cancel your scores from this test administration, you must:
A. fill in both ovals here .... ◯ – ◯   B. sign your full name here: _____

TR	TW	TFS	TCS	1R	1W	1FS	1CS	2R	2W	2FS	2CS
	FOR ETS USE ONLY			3R	3W	3FS	3CS	4R	4W	4FS	4CS
				5R	5W	5FS	5CS	6R	6W	6FS	6CS

GRADUATE RECORD EXAMINATIONS® - GRE® - SUBJECT TEST

DO NOT USE INK

Use only a pencil with soft, black lead (No. 2 or HB) to complete this answer sheet.
Be sure to fill in completely the space that corresponds to your answer choice.
Completely erase any errors or stray marks.

1. NAME
Last Name (Family or Surname) - first 15 letters

Enter your last name, first name initial (given name), and middle initial if you have one. Omit spaces, apostrophes, Jr., II., etc.

2. YOUR NAME:
Last Name (Family or Surname)   First Name (Given)   M.I.
(Print)

MAILING ADDRESS:
P.O. Box or Street Address
City   State or Province
Country   Zip or Postal Code

CENTER:
City   Center Number   Room Number
Country   State or Province

3. DATE OF BIRTH
Month: Jan, Feb, Mar, April, May, June, July, Aug, Sept, Oct, Nov, Dec.
Day | Year

4. SOCIAL SECURITY NUMBER
(U.S.A. only)

5. REGISTRATION NUMBER
(from your admission ticket)

6. TITLE CODE
(from middle of back cover of your test book)

7. TEST NAME
(on back cover of your test book)

8. TEST BOOK SERIAL NUMBER
(red number in upper right corner of front cover of your test book)

FORM CODE (on back cover of your test book)

BE SURE EACH MARK IS DARK AND COMPLETELY FILLS THE INTENDED SPACE AS ILLUSTRATED HERE: ●
YOU MAY FIND MORE RESPONSE SPACES THAN YOU NEED. IF SO, PLEASE LEAVE THEM BLANK.

Questions 1–114: answer choices A B C D E

Item responses continued on reverse side.

SIDE 1

SHADED AREA FOR ETS USE ONLY

SIDE 2

SUBJECT TEST

COMPLETE THE CERTIFICATION STATEMENT, THEN TURN ANSWER SHEET OVER TO SIDE 1.

CERTIFICATION STATEMENT
Please write the following statement below, DO NOT PRINT.
"I certify that I am the person whose name appears on this answer sheet. I also agree not to disclose the contents of the test I am taking today to anyone." Sign and date where indicated.

SIGNATURE: _____ DATE: __/__/__
Month Day Year

BE SURE EACH MARK IS DARK AND COMPLETELY FILLS THE INTENDED SPACE AS ILLUSTRATED HERE: ●
YOU MAY FIND MORE RESPONSE SPACES THAN YOU NEED. IF SO, PLEASE LEAVE THEM BLANK.

Questions 115–242, each with options A B C D E.

IF YOU DO NOT WANT THIS ANSWER SHEET TO BE SCORED

If you want to cancel your scores from this administration, complete A and B below. No record of this test will be sent to the recipients you indicated, and there will be no scores on your GRE file. You will receive confirmation of this cancellation; you will **not** receive scores for this test. Once a score is canceled, it cannot be reinstated.

To cancel your scores from this test administration, you must:

TR	TW	TFS	TCS	1R	1W	1FS	1CS	2R	2W	2FS	2CS
	FOR ETS USE ONLY			3R	3W	3FS	3CS	4R	4W	4FS	4CS
				5R	5W	5FS	5CS	6R	6W	6FS	6CS

GRADUATE RECORD EXAMINATIONS® - GRE® - SUBJECT TEST

DO NOT USE INK

Use only a pencil with soft, black lead (No. 2 or HB) to complete this answer sheet.
Be sure to fill in completely the space that corresponds to your answer choice.
Completely erase any errors or stray marks.

1. NAME

Enter your last name, first name initial (given name), and middle initial if you have one. Omit spaces, apostrophes, Jr., II., etc.

Last Name (Family or Surname) - first 15 letters | F.I. | M.I.

2. YOUR NAME: (Print)
Last Name (Family or Surname)   First Name (Given)   M.I.

MAILING ADDRESS: (Print)
P.O. Box or Street Address
City
State or Province
Country
Zip or Postal Code

CENTER:
City
State or Province
Country
Center Number
Room Number

3. DATE OF BIRTH
Month: Jan., Feb., Mar., April, May, June, July, Aug., Sept., Oct., Nov., Dec.
Day
Year

4. SOCIAL SECURITY NUMBER
(U.S.A. only)

5. REGISTRATION NUMBER
(from your admission ticket)

6. TITLE CODE
(from middle of back cover of your test book)

7. TEST NAME (on back cover of your test book)

FORM CODE (on back cover of your test book)

8. TEST BOOK SERIAL NUMBER
(red number in upper right corner of front cover of your test book)

SHADED AREA FOR ETS USE ONLY

BE SURE EACH MARK IS DARK AND COMPLETELY FILLS THE INTENDED SPACE AS ILLUSTRATED HERE: ●
YOU MAY FIND MORE RESPONSE SPACES THAN YOU NEED. IF SO, PLEASE LEAVE THEM BLANK.

Answer grid: Items 1–114, each with options (A) (B) (C) (D) (E)

Item responses continued on reverse side.

SIDE 1

SIDE 2

SUBJECT TEST

COMPLETE THE CERTIFICATION STATEMENT, THEN TURN ANSWER SHEET OVER TO SIDE 1.

CERTIFICATION STATEMENT
Please write the following statement below, DO NOT PRINT.
"I certify that I am the person whose name appears on this answer sheet. I also agree not to disclose the contents of the test I am taking today to anyone."
Sign and date where indicated.

SIGNATURE: _____ DATE: __/__/__
                                         Month Day Year

BE SURE EACH MARK IS DARK AND COMPLETELY FILLS THE INTENDED SPACE AS ILLUSTRATED HERE: ●.
YOU MAY FIND MORE RESPONSE SPACES THAN YOU NEED. IF SO, PLEASE LEAVE THEM BLANK.

[Answer bubbles numbered 115–242, each with options A B C D E]

IF YOU DO NOT WANT THIS ANSWER SHEET TO BE SCORED

If you want to cancel your scores from this administration, complete A and B below. No record of this test will be sent to the recipients you indicated, and there will be no scores on your GRE file. You will receive confirmation of this cancellation; you will **not** receive scores for this test. Once a score is canceled, it cannot be reinstated.

To cancel your scores from this test administration, you must:
A. fill in both ovals here

TR	TW	TFS	TCS	1R	1W	1FS	1CS	2R	2W	2FS	2CS
				3R	3W	3FS	3CS	4R	4W	4FS	4CS
	FOR ETS USE ONLY										
				5R	5W	5FS	5CS	6R	6W	6FS	6CS

GRADUATE RECORD EXAMINATIONS® - GRE® - SUBJECT TEST

SIDE 1

DO NOT USE INK

Use only a pencil with soft, black lead (No. 2 or HB) to complete this answer sheet.
Be sure to fill in completely the space that corresponds to your answer choice.
Completely erase any errors or stray marks.

1. NAME

Enter your last name, first name initial (given name), and middle initial if you have one.
Omit spaces, apostrophes, Jr., II., etc.

Last Name (Family or Surname) - first 15 letters

2. YOUR NAME:
(Print)

Last Name (Family or Surname) _____ First Name (Given) _____ M.I. _____

MAILING ADDRESS:
(Print)

P.O. Box or Street Address _____

City _____ State or Province _____

Country _____ Zip or Postal Code _____

CENTER:

City _____ State or Province _____

Country _____ Center Number _____ Room Number _____

3. DATE OF BIRTH

Month / Day / Year

Jan., Feb., Mar., April, May, June, July, Aug., Sept., Oct., Nov., Dec.

4. SOCIAL SECURITY NUMBER
(U.S.A. only)

5. REGISTRATION NUMBER
(from your admission ticket)

6. TITLE CODE
(from middle of back cover of your test book)

7. TEST NAME
(on back cover of your test book)

FORM CODE
(on back cover of your test book)

8. TEST BOOK SERIAL NUMBER
(red number in upper right corner of front cover of your test book)

SHADED AREA FOR ETS USE ONLY

BE SURE EACH MARK IS DARK AND COMPLETELY FILLS THE INTENDED SPACE AS ILLUSTRATED HERE: ●
YOU MAY FIND MORE RESPONSE SPACES THAN YOU NEED. IF SO, PLEASE LEAVE THEM BLANK.

Items 1–114: A B C D E

Item responses continued on reverse side.

SIDE 2

SUBJECT TEST

COMPLETE THE CERTIFICATION STATEMENT, THEN TURN ANSWER SHEET OVER TO SIDE 1.

CERTIFICATION STATEMENT
Please write the following statement below, DO NOT PRINT.
"I certify that I am the person whose name appears on this answer sheet. I also agree not to disclose the contents of the test I am taking today to anyone."
Sign and date where indicated.

SIGNATURE: _____ DATE: ___/___/___
                                                                                            Month Day Year

BE SURE EACH MARK IS DARK AND COMPLETELY FILLS THE INTENDED SPACE AS ILLUSTRATED HERE: ●
YOU MAY FIND MORE RESPONSE SPACES THAN YOU NEED. IF SO, PLEASE LEAVE THEM BLANK.

Questions 115–242, each with answer choices A B C D E.

IF YOU DO NOT WANT THIS ANSWER SHEET TO BE SCORED

If you want to cancel your scores from this administration, complete A and B below. No record of this test will be sent to the recipients you indicated, and there will be no scores on your GRE file. You will receive confirmation of this cancellation; you will **not** receive scores for this test. Once a score is canceled, it cannot be reinstated.

To cancel your scores from this test administration, you must:
A. fill in both ovals here .... O – O   B. sign your full name here: _____

TR	TW	TFS	TCS	1R	1W	1FS	1CS	2R	2W	2FS	2CS
	FOR ETS USE ONLY			3R	3W	3FS	3CS	4R	4W	4FS	4CS
				5R	5W	5FS	5CS	6R	6W	6FS	6CS